Greywater Use in the Middle East

University of Stirling

Praise for the book...

'Greywater use may not solve the water crisis, but this book sheds light and important research on its potential to contribute something to the solution. It proposes information and technological solutions to both reduce the stigma associated with greywater use, while providing straightforward options to policy makers.'

Eglal Rached is the Cairo Regional Director, IDRC

'Greywater is a recognized vital irrigation supply source here in Southern Arizona. We have come a significant distance from the days when greywater use was forbidden.

This new comprehensive reference provides a compelling argument for the use of greywater in the Middle East providing the varied expertise and experience required for its safe and practical use in a single, concise document; this is clearly a positive step forward. Hopefully, this book will lead to further funded research and demonstration projects that address its questions and preliminary conclusions.'

Professor Richard Brittain, Department of Architecture,
University of Arizona

'This book is timely in many ways: timely, because of the increasing problem of freshwater scarcity in many parts of the world; timely, because the resilience of our water supply and hydraulic systems in the face of climate change is in question; timely, because the health, livelihood and nutritional status of peri-urban populations are under threat. The book's specific focus takes greywater out of the shadow of wastewater and excreta use in agriculture and highlights new opportunities to contribute to poverty alleviation.'

Robert Bos, World Health Organization,
Department of Public Health and Environment

Greywater Use in the Middle East
Technical, Social, Economic and Policy Issues

Z
28.3
MCL

POP

Edited by
Stephen McIlwaine and Mark Redwood

Center for the Study of
the Built Environment

International Development Research Centre
Ottawa • Cairo • Dakar • Montevideo • Nairobi • New Delhi • Singapore

06/10

Practical Action Publishing Ltd
Schumacher Centre for Technology and Development
Bourton on Dunsmore, Rugby,
Warwickshire, CV23 9QZ, UK
www.practicalactionpublishing.org

ISBN 978 1 85339 698 4

and the International Development Research Centre
P.O. Box 8500, Ottawa, ON, Canada K1G 3HP
www.idrc.ca/info@idrc.ca

ISBN 978 1 55250 466 6 (e-book)

and the Center for the Study of the Built Environment (CSBE)
PO Box: 830751, Amman 11183, Jordan
www.csbe.org

Since 1974, Practical Action Publishing (formerly Intermediate Technology
Publications and ITDG Publishing) has published and disseminated books
and information in support of international development work throughout
the world. Practical Action Publishing Ltd (Company Reg. No. 1159018)
is the wholly owned publishing company of Practical Action Ltd. Practical
Action Publishing trades only in support of its parent charity objectives and
any profits are covenanted back to Practical Action (Charity Reg. No. 247257,
Group VAT Registration No. 880 9924 76).

Cover photo: Mr Othman Abdallah Al-Amer of Ariha village, Karak, Jordan,
inspects the confined trench (CT) unit in his garden. Credit: Murad J. Bino.

Cover design by Practical Action Publishing
Indexed by Andrea Palmer
Typeset by S.J.I. Services
Printed by Replika Press, India

Contents

Figures   vii

Tables   ix

Foreword   xi
HE Dr Munther Haddadin, former Minister of Water and Irrigation, Jordan

Preface   xiii
Stephen McIlwaine and Mark Redwood

The Aqaba Declaration on Greywater Use   xv

Acknowledgements   xvii

Acronyms and abbreviations   xix

1. Introduction: Greywater use in the Middle East – the story so far   1
   Mark Redwood

PART I: TECHNICAL ASPECTS

2. On-site greywater treatment in Qebia Village, Palestine   17
   Jamal Burnat and Intissar Eshtayah

3. Greywater use in rural home gardens in Karak, Jordan   29
   Murad Bino, Shihab Al-Beiruti and Mohammad Ayesh

4. Greywater management in the northeastern Badia of Jordan   59
   Wael Suleiman, Bassam Al-Hayek, Moayied Assayed, Sahar Dalahmeh and Nisreen Al-Hmoud

PART II: SOCIOECONOMIC ASPECTS

5. Stakeholder participation in greywater management in the Jordanian Badia   77
   Sahar Dalahmeh, Moayied Assayed, Wael Suleiman and Bassam Al-Hayek

6. Comparative socioeconomic study of greywater and cesspit systems in Ramallah, Palestine   89
   Maher Abu-Madi, Rashed Al-Sa'ed, Nidal Mahmoud and Jamal Burnat

7. Can local people accept greywater technology?   101
    Peter Laban

8. Lessons from a participatory approach to household greywater
    use in Jordan   113
    Noel Keough, Samira Smira and Stan Benjamin

9. Greywater use as a gender empowerment project in Tannoura,
    Lebanon   129
    Nadine Haddad El-Hajj

10. Greywater use: Islamic perspectives   139
    Odeh Al-Jayyousi

PART III: POLICY ISSUES AND NEXT STEPS

11. Policy and regulatory approaches to greywater use in the
    Middle East   151
    Stephen McIlwaine

12. Conclusion: Next steps for research, policy and implementation   165
    Mark Redwood, Stephen McIlwaine and Marwan Owaygen

Index   173

Figures

1.1 The Stockholm Framework for the assessment of health risk   5

2.1 Septic tank–up-flow gravel filter treatment unit   20

2.2 Final stage greywater filtration   20

2.3 Fresh greywater polluting home garden soil   22

3.1 Two-barrel greywater treatment unit   32

3.2 Four-barrel greywater treatment unit   32

3.3 Confined trench greywater treatment unit   33

3.4 Circular concrete greywater treatment unit   33

3.5 Rectangular concrete greywater treatment unit   34

4.1 Septic tank–sand filter unit   70

4.2 Up-flow anaerobic sludge blanket (UASB) reactor   70

5.1 Stakeholder information flow   81

Tables

0.1   Participants in the Aqaba Declaration on Greywater Use   xvi

2.1   Methods of analysis   21

2.2   Characteristics of untreated greywater from the Qebia Project   23

3.1   Quality of raw greywater from representative houses   40

3.2   Quality of treated greywater from four-barrel and CT units monitored between December 2006 and September 2007   42

3.3   Variations of raw and treated greywater   43

3.4   Results of analysis of heavy metals in a household greywater effluent   43

3.5   Properties of soil not subject to greywater irrigation   43

3.6   Olive yield increase due to irrigation with greywater, 2007   43

3.7   Results of monitoring greywater impacts on soil EC, SAR, and soil organic matter content   44

3.8   Results of chemical analysis of plants irrigated with treated greywater during 2007   45

3.9   Results of microbiological analysis of plants and soils irrigated with treated greywater during 2007   45

3.10   Effects of mulching on soil content of nutrients and CaCO3 (2007)   46

3.11   Effects of soil mulching and rain harvesting on soil salinity (2007)   46

3.12   Capital costs of greywater treatment units (based on 2006 Jordan prices)   50

3.13   Average net present costs for the 60 surveyed houses   51

3.14   Average net present benefits (present revenues – present costs) per family   51

3.15   Average net present benefits (present revenues – present costs) for four different scenarios   52

3.16   Average values of the benefit–cost ratios for different scenarios   52

4.1   Population distribution (2001)   60

4.2   Checklist prepared and used by the local stakeholder committee   62

4.3   Greywater quality generated at different discharge points   66

4.4   Selection matrix of the greywater treatment system   68

4.5   Selection matrix of the greywater treatment system (cont'd)   69

4.6   Performance of septic tank/sand filter system   71

4.7   Performance of UASB/zeolite system   71

4.8   Cost–benefit analysis of UASB treatment unit   72

4.9   Cost–benefit analysis of septic tank/sand filter treatment unit   72

5.1   Treatment technology evaluation criteria   84

5.2   Design criteria for the treatment systems   84

6.1   CAPEX comparison of GWS and cesspits   93

6.2   OPEX comparison of GWS and cesspits per household unit   93

6.3   Impact of GWS and cesspits on households' expenditure on
       water and wastewater   94

6.4   Benefit–cost ratio of GWS   95

Foreword

The formal treatment and use of wastewater began in the Middle East in the late 1960s, firstly in Jordan, and soon after in Israel. The need to formalize a policy for that practice became pressing in 1978 when supplies of municipal water in Amman became short. This saw a high-level decision to divert surface freshwater earmarked for agriculture to municipal uses in Amman, and led to the compensation of agriculture with treated municipal wastewater. This was the beginning of my involvement in the topic of the use of treated wastewater.

In 1988, the World Bank invited myself and a colleague to carry out a study of wastewater use and evaluate its economic, social and public health feasibility for water strained countries. That initiative was soon followed by a joint IBRD–UNDP–FAO–WHO (International Bank for Reconstruction and Development–United Nations Development Programme–Food and Agriculture Organziation–World Health Organziation) mission to countries in the Middle East to evaluate the practice of, and the potential for, using treated wastewater. By that stage, wastewater was already being used in Yemen, Saudi Arabia, Jordan and Syria and was planned for Cyprus, Egypt and Turkey. The impact that this reclaimed resource had on the sustainability of agriculture, especially in the Jordan Valley and the Ghuta of Damascus, where agricultural water had been diverted to municipal uses, was undeniable. In 1997–98, as Minister of Water and Irrigation of Jordan, I formulated Jordan's Wastewater Management Policy which considered wastewater as a resource, not as a waste.

Greywater is one component of wastewater that has not yet received its due attention. Latcly, countries in our region are becoming more aware of the potential of greywater, both for irrigation and landscaping as well as for other uses. The use of greywater in poor rural areas can be both socially and economically rewarding. If the 'polluter pays' principle applies, one can justify, on environmental grounds, the subsidy that society should make to enable the treatment of raw wastewater to render it environmentally acceptable, with land application as the optimum disposal method.

I believe it is already overdue that the scientific and professional water community and officials in charge pay closer attention to the use of greywater. This book is a loud knock on their doors that it may seriously begin.

Dr Munther Haddadin
Former Minister of Water and Irrigation, Jordan

Preface

This book follows a meeting held in Aqaba, Jordan, in 2007 and convened by the International Development Research Centre (IDRC) and the Centre for the Study of the Built Environment (CSBE). At that time, an effort was made to come to a consensus on what are the priority issues associated with greywater use, what kind of work existed on greywater use in the Middle East and North Africa (MENA) region, and where research could make further contributions. A series of projects on greywater use in home agriculture pursued by regional research institutes, such as the Inter-Islamic Network on Water Resources Development and Management (INWRDAM), the Palestinian Agricultural Relief Committees (PARC), and Birzeit University, were reviewed covering the years 1999–2007. In all, 35 participants attended, representing 17 different institutions, and were asked the following questions:

- What have we learned from these projects?
- How do we balance the economic and environmental benefits of greywater with the need to mitigate the potential health and environmental risks?
- How can we raise the profile of greywater amongst policy makers and promote its widespread use?

The meeting concluded by formulating and agreeing a statement summarizing participants' concerns and aspirations regarding greywater research and implementation. This Aqaba Declaration on Greywater Use is reproduced below.

This book is a compilation of the learning that was acquired through these projects and reflections on what managed greywater use may contribute to water conservation. Moreover, given the 2006 publication of the *WHO Guidelines for the Safe Use of Wastewater, Excreta and Greywater*, the time is ripe for a renewed look at greywater.

The main conclusion of the efforts spent in researching greywater is that while its contribution to macro or regional water conservation will always be modest, it can nevertheless ease some of the more extreme exposure to problems of poverty resulting from water scarcity. We do not want to exaggerate the potential for greywater; it can not be a panacea for the crisis of water management. However, the mere fact that it is being practiced merits attention from researchers to maximize its benefits and reduce any associated risks. In addition to the use of greywater for agriculture, there are potential uses at a larger scale, for toilet flushing and landscaping, but these are not dealt with in this volume.

We are concerned for the future of water use in the MENA region. Without better demand management, the supply-oriented and technology-driven approach to meeting water needs will not deliver what is required to balance needs with the available resources. Excessive efforts by the authorities to regulate greywater use will miss the point that more effort is required at all levels to ensure that water is used efficiently, that it is reused wherever possible, and that its intrinsic value be reflected in policy.

Greywater is one small contribution to supplement the incomes of some of the poor in water-scarce environments and under controlled conditions it becomes another tool in the battle to reduce water waste.

Stephen McIlwaine and Mark Redwood

The Aqaba Declaration on Greywater Use

We, 29 experts, researchers, and practitioners from eight different countries and representing 17 institutions agree that greywater provides an important potential to alleviate water scarcity in dry countries and that it should be seen as a water source as opposed to a waste product. We also agree that the use of reclaimed greywater can be environmentally, socially, and economically beneficial and culturally acceptable.

We consider that greywater use must be promoted in a way that minimizes health and environmental risks while generating economic benefits.

Based on what is known to date, we also agree that greywater use is considered to have potential as a water demand management option for the MENA region and that we should respond to existing demand for non-conventional sources of water by promoting the widespread adoption of greywater use.

It is useful to see greywater both as a strategy to address water scarcity, as well as a poverty alleviation strategy.

In order to raise the profile of greywater and promote its widespread use we need to work closely with all relevant stakeholders and should focus on clear and straightforward messages.

We agree that more information is required, for example on:

- the impacts of greywater use on health;
- the impacts of greywater use on soil and plants;
- the social and economic impact;
- greywater characterization;
- appropriate technologies.

We agree that any technological intervention should be cost effective while meeting accepted standards.

Table 0.1 Participants in the Aqaba Declaration on Greywater Use

Name	Institution
Mark Redwood	International Development Research Centre (IDRC), Canada
Dr Stephen McIlwaine	Center for the Study of the Built Environment (CSBE), Jordan
Dr Murad J. Bino	Inter-Islamic Network on Water Resources Development and Management (INWRDAM), Jordan
Dr Odeh Al-Jayyousi	The World Conservation Union (IUCN)
Wael Suleiman	Royal Scientific Society (RSS), Jordan
Dr Fadhl Al Nozaily	Water and Environment Centre (WEC), University of Sana'a, Yemen
Rania Abdel Khaleq	Ministry of Water and Irrigation (MoWI), Jordan
Jamal Burnat	Agricultural Cooperative Development International and Volunteers in Overseas Cooperative Assistance (ACDI-VOCA), Palestinian Territories
Intissar Fshtayah	Palestinian Wastewater Engineers Group (PWEG), Palestinian Territories
Nadine Haddad El-Hajj	Middle East Centre for the Transfer of Appropriate Technology (MECTAT), Lebanon
Dr Maher Abu-Madi	Birzeit University, Palestinian Territories
Monther Hind	PWEG, Palestinian Territories
Dr Noel Keough	PLAN:NET, Canada
Dr Cecilia Oman	International Foundation for Science (IFS), Sweden
Peter Laban	CARE/EMPOWERS, Palestinian Territories
Shihab Al-Beiruti	INWRDAM, Jordan
Dr Marwan Owaygen	IDRC, Canada
Lorra Thompson	IDRC, Canada
Karma El-Fadl	CSBE, Jordan
Silke Rothenberger	SANDEC, Switzerland
Boghos Ghougassian	MECTAT, Lebanon
Marieke Adank	IRC – International Water and Sanitation Centre, Netherlands
Moath Asfour	INWRDAM, Jordan
Mohammad Ayesh	National Centre for Agricultural Research and Technology Transfer (NCARTT), Jordan
Mufeed Batarseh	Mutah University, Jordan
Moayied Assayed	RSS, Jordan
Sahar Dalahmeh	RSS, Jordan
Samira Smirat	PLAN:NET, Jordan
Abd Al Razzaq Abu Rahman	Palestinian Hydrology Group (PHG), Palestinian Territories

Acknowledgements

The editors would like to thank the Review Committee who provided valuable comments on the material: Dr Murad Bino, Inter-Islamic Network on Water Resources Development and Management (INW-RDAM), Amman, Jordan, Dr Noel Keough, PLAN:NET Ltd, Canada and Dr Mushtaque Ahmad, Sultan Qaboos University, Muscat, Oman.

In addition, thanks are due to Christopher Scott, University of Arizona, for comments on the text, to Karen Hanson and Sawsan Zaater who assisted with the technical editing of some of the material and Nur al-Fayez who assisted with preparation of the images. Particular thanks are due to Majd Musa, who persevered with the final proofreading and stylistic editing of the manuscript.

Acronyms and abbreviations

ACDI-VOCA	Agricultural Cooperative Development International and Volunteers in Overseas Cooperative Assistance
BOD	Biological oxygen demand
BOD_5	Biological oxygen demand at 5 days
CAPEX	Capital/investment expenditures
CBOs	Community-based organizations
CIDA	Canadian International Development Agency
CLs	Community leaders
COD	Chemical oxygen demand
DFID	Department for International Development (UK)
EC	Electrical conductivity (a measure of salinity)
E. coli	*Escherichia coli*
FOG	Fat, oil and grease
GW	Greywater
GWS	Greywater system(s)
GWT	Greywater treatment
IDRC	International Development Research Centre
ISF	Intermittent sand filter
IWRM	Integrated Water Resource Management
LSC	Local stakeholder committee
MBAS	Methyl blue active substance
MPN	Most probable number
NGOs	Non-governmental organizations
OPEX	Operational expenditures
PARC	Palestinian Agricultural Relief Committees
PHG	Palestinian Hydrology Group
PRA	Participatory rural (or rapid) appraisal
PWEG	Palestinian Wastewater Engineers Group
SC	Save the Children
TDS	Total dissolved solids
T Kj N	Total Kjeldahl nitrogen

T-N	Total nitrogen
T-P	Total phosphorous
TSS	Total suspended solid
UASB	Up-flow anaerobic sludge blanket
UN	United Nations
USAID	United States Agency for International Development
WaDImena	Water Demand Initiative in the Middle East and North Africa

CHAPTER 1

Introduction: Greywater use in the Middle East – the story so far

Mark Redwood

Background and context

Freshwater scarcity is an environmental fact in the Middle East and North Africa (MENA) region. Home to 5 per cent of the world's population, the region only contains 1 per cent of accessible water resources. In the MENA region, per capita water availability hovers around 1,200 m^3 per capita/year whereas the global average is 7,000 m^3 per capita/year (World Bank, 2008). With population growth taken into account, it is predicted that per capita water availability in the region will halve by 2050. The water that does exist is concentrated in a few areas such as the Nile River and the Fertile Crescent. Even though agriculture accounts for most water use, an increasing proportion of freshwater is being used by cities (UN-Habitat, 2008). The MENA region is also faced with geopolitical problems that naturally end up affecting natural-resource equity. For instance, water stress in the Palestinian Territories is compounded by problems associated with geopolitics (Homer-Dixon, 1994). Some countries such as the Gulf states have virtually no surface water to speak of and are reliant on groundwater or desalination.

Meanwhile, there are problems of access to adequate sanitation in many underserved areas in the MENA region. A serious challenge in some poorer urban and rural areas relates to access to basic collection services for waste. As Abu-Madi and colleagues point out in this volume (Chapter 6), only 25 per cent of Palestinian households in the territories are privy to centralized sewerage while only 6 per cent of all wastewater is actually treated.

As freshwater becomes increasingly scarce, it is necessary to shift attention to alternative sources of water, particularly for the rural and peri-urban poor. A few shining examples of conservation and waste recycling exist. For instance in Jordan, Tunisia, and Israel, controlled wastewater use is practiced with significant impact on those countries' water budgets. Outside the MENA region, other countries have employed a proactive policy of reclaiming wastewater for productive use including the USA (California and Arizona) and Australia (Redwood, 2008b).

Recycling wastewater for food production is less common than using wastewater for municipal uses, golf courses, or wetlands. Yet, it is common in poorer

countries of the world where water is simply unavailable or where the economic incentive to reuse is substantial. It is estimated that 20 million farmers
worldwide use untreated or partially treated wastewater (WHO, 2008).

The common definition of greywater refers to it as wastewater derived
from kitchens, bathrooms, and laundry water, but excluding toilets (known
as 'black water') (Redwood, 2008b). Greywater (GW) thus does not contain
the same elevated level of pathogens (WHO, 2006). That said, some argue
that GW originating in kitchens – and thus with a high organic load – can
contain high levels of waste and thus pose an unacceptable risk of pathogenic
contamination (Casanova et al., 2001). Greywater is also an area of study for
which there is still only limited consensus; some are not convinced of its value
given the potential risks, while others see GW as one contribution to water
conservation (Noah, 2002). The principle issue is not to view GW in terms of
achieving substantial water savings, but rather, view the potential of GW to
make modest improvements in income among those who use it.

Underlining research around GW are several realities. First, as noted above,
the MENA region is faced with a dire need for alternative sources of water.
It is not possible to overstate this need. Second, GW is already being used
by many farmers in an uncontrolled way. The best estimate we have as to
the prevalence of GW use comes from the Department of Statistics in Jordan
whose 2001 Amman census revealed that 40 per cent of the population use
GW, to some extent, to irrigate their gardens (DOS, 2001). This amounts to
500,000 people in the city alone. The main reasons for the use of GW are the
potential nutrient benefits leading to increased harvests, as well as savings in
terms of fertilizer and water costs (WHO, 2006). It can safely be said that the
proportion of use may be higher in rural areas where access to potable water
and sanitation is more infrequent.

Third, a number of jurisdictions outside the MENA region have developed
policies on GW use. These policies can be simple and straightforward and are
being applied (see for example, McIlwaine, Chapter 11 in this volume). We
are convinced that with appropriate knowledge on the origins, quality and
practices associated with GW, the same potential of its use can be released for
MENA. Although low-cost treatment options that negate health risks and improve the quality of GW exist, agreement is still elusive on what kinds of low-
cost technologies are feasible within certain social and economic contexts.
In other words, we need to answer the question of what would drive farmers
already using GW to apply even a simple practice or technical solution to reduce health risk, when they may not see this intervention as necessary.

Fourth, much of the work associated with GW use – especially treatment
– is site specific. This suggests that there is a potential for mitigation and some
opportunities that planners and managers may be able to take advantage of to
maximize the benefits and minimize the risks associated with GW use.

Finally, the consensus is clear that wastewater use under controlled conditions is now an accepted and responsible method of achieving water savings.
The 2006 *WHO Guidelines for the Safe Use of Wastewater, Excreta and Greywater*

clearly state that GW 'contains nutrients and water, which make them valuable resources' (vol. 4: 8), a point that underscores the entire effort to research what can be done to capture its value.

Greywater use as a water demand management strategy

Underlining the debate around the use of marginal quality and wastewater is a conservationist principle. The Dublin Principles, for example, point to not only the essential inherent value of water (Principle 1) but also to the importance of seeing it as an economic good that can be considered scarce (Principle 4). The broad principle of 'getting the most use out of the water we have' is known as water demand management, and means simply that one tries to maximize the efficiency of use of a resource in order to avoid requiring new supplies. When applied to water, this means using wastewater, conservation measures to reduce consumption and price points that encourage less use of the resource. In countries with large sources of capital, an over reliance on groundwater and desalination continues to support the conventional 'supply-side' approach – an unsustainable answer to this regions' deep environmental crisis (IDRC, 2009). Greywater use is thus a water-demand management strategy however modest its contribution.

Estimates of household water savings are dependent on climate, household income, and cultural preferences. Otterpohl (2002) proposes a range of estimates from 75 litres per household per day (l/hh/day) in some countries to 275 l/hh/day in others. It is more difficult to extrapolate how these household water savings end up impacting on national water budgets. The literature contains few scientific analyses of the actual potential for GW to respond to the regional water budget. Friedler (2008) conducted one piece of research that analysed the potential for the penetration of GW use in Israel. He suggests that it is feasible, given social, economic, and cultural circumstances to have on-site GW use 'penetration' in 19–31 per cent of Israel. This potential would be the equivalent of annual water savings totalling the annual demand of a small city of 400,000 residents. While no comparative study has been done for neighbouring countries in MENA, this research suggests that the potential savings are considerable, but only a partial response to the way water is inefficiently used.

Are health and safety issues the primary question?

The reluctance of policy makers and attached social stigma has played a key role in preventing the successful and widespread adoption of GW as a water-use strategy. However, there is also a great deal of misunderstanding about the ease with which GW can be managed safely. The fear of risk, in a sense, has paralysed and prohibited many good and practical ideas for managing GW safely for use from being acted upon. The WHO guidelines point out that 'bacterial indicators tend to overestimate the faecal load in greywater' due to the fact that regrowth can occur. However, 'the microbial contamination... must be taken into account when calculating risks and selecting treatment methods' (WHO, 2006: vol. 4).

The net benefit of reusing nutrient-rich wastewater for application on land crops is clearly positive, especially if the alternative is to dump the waste into rivers, streams, and other surface water (EAWAG, 2006). Greywater is less nutrient-rich than toilet wastewater containing excreta, but nevertheless is a source of phosphorous (from laundry water) and nitrogen (from kitchen waste). If redirected to irrigation, these nutrients can help plant growth. If they are disposed of in surface water they can cause serious environmental problems such as algae blooms and eutrophication, which accounts for efforts by policy makers to reduce or eliminate the presence of phosphates in some cleaners.

The 2006 WHO guidelines: A significant shift in perspective

Until 2006, guidelines for wastewater and GW use were adapted from the *Guidelines for the Safe Use of Wastewater and Excreta in Agriculture and Aquaculture*, published by WHO in 1989 (Mara and Cairncross, 1989). The guidelines offered a programming framework for management, as well as a straightforward set of numerical guidelines related to faecal coliform (FC) counts and Helminth Eggs. One failure of the 1989 guidelines was the misinterpretation of numerical guidelines as standards. This problem contributed to a reassessment of how to approach the development of new guidelines on wastewater uses, which are embodied in the 2006 WHO guidelines (WHO, 2006). The three key elements put forward by the guidelines are:

- evidence-based health risk assessment;
- guidance for managing risk (including options other than wastewater treatment);
- strategies for guideline implementation (including progressive implementation where necessary).

The 2006 WHO guidelines do not exaggerate concern about GW. Instead, their response is pragmatic: policy and planning for GW use must be done with consideration of the local health context in which GW is being used. So, in a country where the major disease burden comes from failed sanitation or easy exposure to sewage, GW use may be a moot point given the relatively low comparative risk. An important change is that the guidelines no longer look at water quality standards, but instead, look at health-based targets. For example, questions such as what level of pathogens are permissible to ingest in light of the possible risk of infection given the health context where the wastewater is being applied (Mara and Kramer, 2008). The incidence of disease caused by wastewater is not only related to exposure, but also to the degree of exposure, the health, and age of those affected. As a result, controls related to the end-use of the recycled wastewater are most effective. The guidelines were refined further by including specific information regarding GW; a tacit acknowledgement that the risks associated with GW are not as severe as those related to combined wastewater.

Additional emphasis is made in the guidelines to develop a risk management approach that is adapted to their own cultural, social, economic and environmental contexts (see Figure 1.1). This common-sense conclusion reflects a big change from the 1989 guidelines, which inadvertently were interpreted as a 'one-size-fits-all' approach. The new guidelines, however, have not proven to be an easy sell, as some note that in the drive to make the guidelines more context-specific, they have had to sacrifice simplicity (Mara and Kramer, 2008). On the other hand, the guidelines are designed in a rolling fashion to be developed in accordance with the latest available data. Recent research has begun to examine the application of this approach in several developing country contexts.[1]

An important component of the guidelines is the notion of a multi-barrier approach to the mitigation of health risks. This approach suggests a series of barriers along the chain of use (both treatment and non-treatment) that can be used to reduce health risks. When applied to GW, simple techniques such as contact avoidance and cessation of irrigation two days prior to harvesting can be effective at eliminating any potential risk (that might be caused by cross contamination, for instance). Slightly more sophisticated options such as constructed wetlands, waste stabilization ponds among others (see below) can offer feasible technological responses to improve the quality of GW. The key point is that mitigation measures should be adapted in coherence with the potential risk. To use highly sophisticated measures to reduce health risks associated with GW adds unnecessary cost.

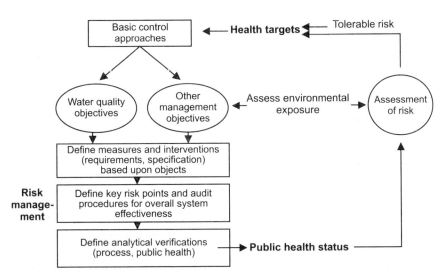

Figure 1.1 The Stockholm Framework for the assessment of health risk (adapted from the WHO 2006 guidelines)

There is ample and growing research that identifies numerous simple methods to control contact with GW and/or treat effluent (WHO, 2008; Otterpohl, 2002). Some simple methods that will reduce risk at the household/farm level include systems such as sand filters, drip irrigation, soil infiltration and constructed wetlands (WHO, 2006). The inclusion of kitchen water as GW is debated since organic matter and soaps can lead to high BOD (biological oxygen demand) and COD (chemical oxygen demand) making treatment more complicated. Ashour and Jamrah (2008) illustrated that kitchen *E. coli* survived in soil irrigated with GW for longer than soil irrigated with GW excluding kitchen waste. It is thus tempting to conclude that kitchen waste should simply not be used unless it is possible to significantly reduce or eliminate the entrance of organic matter.

Environmental impacts

Given the prevalence of household chemical use, it is not unusual to assume that GW can have a harmful environmental impact. Chemical pollutants, in particular, can be serious. Laundry detergents are a source of boron (B) and surfactants. Boron can be toxic to plants in large quantities while surfactants can alter soil properties if highly concentrated. Some research has shown that GW contains high concentrations of these components (Gross et al., 2005). Surfactant content in GW suggests that application of GW – even if treated – can damage soil in the long term (Gross et al., 2008). The promotion of environmentally friendly detergents and/or the mixing of freshwater with GW used in agriculture are some responses to this conundrum, again with the view of improving the influent.

Most research suggests that household detergents and chemicals render GW as 'generally unfit' for use except when controlled, given the suggested long-term impact on soil (Carden et al., 2005; Wiel-Shafran et al., 2006). In developing country contexts and where household GW is used to supplement the immediacy of a low-income household, this is not a particularly useful conclusion. Moreover, other authors have pointed to the very limited data on the long-term impact of GW on soil and crops, which makes continued research necessary before drawing any concrete conclusions (Redwood, 2008b).

Is there a need for greywater treatment?

It is a fallacy that treatment is ultimately necessary in order to reduce the risks associated with GW use. In fact, despite the evidence of some effective household-level treatment options in this volume there are many who believe treatment is necessary. Most arguments stem from two facts. First, GW can be relatively benign and it is not necessary to treat it to the same degree as combined wastewater. Second, decentralized treatment frequently fails to take into account the difficulty in operating and managing at a small scale (Lens et al., 2001).

Ultimately, there are two things that matter most: that appropriate technology is used, and that the existence of interest and technical capacity to manage such technology is readily available. A more sophisticated approach to management, including pre-treatment and household-level options, has not been shown to be economically feasible in the short term (Redwood, 2008a).

The end-use matters!

Requirements for GW management are highly dependent on end-use. EAWAG (2006) suggests that primary treatment is adequate, since irrigated soil acts as a good secondary treatment and contributes to pathogen die-off. Also, the parameters for acceptable wastewater quality have generally been taken from the 1989 WHO guidelines, which have wrongly been interpreted as standards thus rendering them inappropriate for most developing-country contexts. The new WHO guidelines (2006) suggest a shift from looking exclusively at treatment to health-based targets where treatment is only one option to achieve the targets.

Many different technologies have been tested for their effectiveness in treating GW. Pidou and colleagues (2007) provide a comprehensive overview to date of current research on different treatment options. These include simple systems involving sedimentation, screening, and disinfection, physical treatment (sand filters and membranes), chemical treatment (coagulation, activated carbon), biological treatment (bio-films, anaerobic filters), and extensive treatment (using constructed wetlands, reed beds, floating macrophytes). Constructed wetlands have been proven to be highly effective at improving GW quality for use. However, these may not be suitable for arid climates due to problems associated with water loss (IWA Specialist Group, 2000).

All management options are faced with the same challenges: cost, ease of use, space and public acceptance. At the core of any GW policy must be enabling factors, or incentives, that would increase the adoption of GW use. All in all, there is a discernible shift from a treatment-centred approach to agreement that treatment may simply not be necessary provided there are other non-treatment options considered. Drawing lessons from stringent policy environments such as Australia, who have opted for a more pragmatic policy approach, would be a good point of departure in MENA.

Policy and social issues

Good governance implies that all of the stakeholders affected by a particular decision will be consulted and informed about the decision in question. Ideally, good science and research should inform such decisions and policy should not be fear driven. In practice, this is not often the case. Greywater is lumped into the general category of combined wastewater without consideration for the fact that it is much less dangerous from a health standpoint. Policy is therefore driven by the fear of the risks associated with such changes.

Treatment is often seen as the best way to improve water quality to an acceptable standard. Unfortunately, much work on GW has proven to be overly technologically-driven and with possible limited uptake without the availability of significant external resources. This tendency ignores the fact that there is social and cultural resistance to GW (and especially combined wastewater) use. In South Africa, fears about appearance and quality have led to some hesitation in its use (Armitage et al., 2009), while in the MENA region, Islamic traditions have limited its welcome adoption due to traditional attitudes. Recent literature and religious decrees make a strong case for the acceptance of the use of wastewaters if they meet accepted norms for quality (Faruqui and Bino, 2001; Al-Damkhi, 2008). Moreover, in this volume, Al-Jayyousi (Chapter 10) points out that water conservation (and GW use) writ large is highly consistent with Islamic principles.

From the technical/policy angle, the main issue regarding GW is of course how to use it safely. Unfortunately, fears for public health often overstate the risks associated with GW and promote a 'no-risk' approach. This is counter productive since it ignores the reality of the many reasons that exist for GW to be used. Furthermore, in developing countries, prohibitive policy simply does not work since few resources exist for enforcement and the incentive to reuse is often an important determinant (income, for instance).

The quality of GW is directly linked with what enters the systems. Therefore household behaviour should be an important part of any strategy to promote or control GW use. Policy can be oriented towards punitive measures that prohibit GW use based on the negative characteristics that have been outlined here, or it can focus on changing behaviour and provide incentive-based guidelines to encourage changes at the household level that will improve effluent quality. In support of the clear behavioural component of wastewater use practices, municipalities increasingly allocate a portion of city budgets associated with sanitation for social interventions (Armitage et al., 2009).

Another factor increasingly exposed is the dichotomy between expert-led agreement on health risks and water policy, on the one hand, and public perceptions and acceptance on the other (Stenekes et al., 2006). Many experts, or technologists, believe that with proven technologies in existence, the only question is how to educate lay people into adopting these approaches. In fact, meaningful public engagement and economic factors are likely to be much more important drivers of change (Redwood, 2008b). Laban (Chapter 7 in this volume) insists that public acceptance of technology is the cornerstone to the successful adoption of GW use at the household level, a perspective that the editors of this book fully agree with. He proposes that Participatory Technology Development (PTD) be adopted to increase citizen uptake of options to treat GW to the point where it is safe to use. It is also worth noting that GW use can be very site specific and user dependent – issues that could be easily handled using PTD.

Policy development on GW use has largely been concentrated in arid regions in developed countries. For example, the State of Arizona, USA, and several Australian municipalities have developed GW use policies. Most responses have exaggerated the risks and over complicated solutions (i.e. treatment technology being a requirement or simply banning its use). However these examples illustrate that simple and flexible options to reduce risk can be promoted through common-sense policy-making. If a policy is overly complex, it will simply be ignored. This may be because costs to comply are too high, or it is simply too complicated to have any meaningful impact on behaviour.

In Arizona, a cornerstone of the policy is that it is applied in reasonable proportion to the threat posed by GW (see McIlwaine, Chapter 11 in this volume). This is in concert with the WHO principle that the threat should not be overstated and that all policy must be adopted based on context-specific data. This important concept is often ignored since absolute intolerance of risk seems to be the rule rather than a more rational approach that accepts that some risks are unknown. Rules are based around avoiding direct contact, prohibiting GW use through spray irrigation, and not allowing crops that are produced for food to be irrigated by surface irrigation (with GW).

Certain examples exist of modifications to building codes in order to increase water and energy use efficiency. Retrofitting homes for the separation of grey- and blackwater can be expensive and is not necessarily a feasible strategy. However in Australia, the Building and Sustainability Index for new developments in Adelaide and Sydney is mandating new developments to meet certain targets associated with water-use efficiency including GW use. Therefore, new homes are being built with waste use in mind. A further inexpensive option is to landscape around buildings with sub-surface GW use in mind (EAWAG, 2006), to use, in other words, constructed wetlands.

Economic and sustainability issues

Of course, any change in behaviour will require some understanding of the economic benefits in order to promote such a change. A review of peer-reviewed literature finds a good deal of work on Integrated Water Resource Management (IWRM) and combined wastewater, but very little that directly applies to economic analysis associated with GW. In short, scientists agree on the potential and pitfalls, but few have figured out what the costs will be. A study of household treatment systems and GW use in Jordan found a cost–benefit ratio of 1 to 1.83 over five years assuming a discount rate of 3 per cent (Bino et al., Chapter 3 this volume). This is not an adequate short-term incentive that would entail widespread behaviour change. Memon and colleagues (2005) point out that the slow uptake of GW treatment systems are directly related to the poor cost–benefit ratio. Without a compelling economic argument, it is highly unlikely that there will be a widespread adoption of GW treatment. This does not mean that GW is not viable, only that more sophisticated economic models are required to understand the externalities associated with GW disposal in order to factor in the full costs associated with waste versus reuse. Using a whole life cost model is the only way to help decision makers effectively implement and market GW treatment and use (Memon et al., 2005; Redwood, 2008b). The need for a comprehensive cost–benefit analysis is acute as to date, mostly descriptive economic data has been presented in the literature.

Other social issues are also critical if GW is to be included in IWRM. Haddad El-Hajj (Chapter 9 in this volume) presents the importance of the role of women in household management and argues that by controlling GW production and use in the home, women in conservative rural communities can manage some aspects of household economic production. Whereas some have suggested caution when applying policy of use of wastewater – even GW – in Islamic countries, Al-Jayyousi (Chapter 10 in this volume) points out that the use of GW is not contradictory to fundamental tenants of Islam. In fact, he suggests that the Islamic principle of *ijtihad* encourages innovation in finding acceptable solutions to new environmental problems.

Serious problems of uptake are noted in this volume by Abu-Madi et al. (Chapter 6), Haddad El-Hajj (Chapter 9), and Bino et al. (Chapter 3). These are associated with the cultural and social acceptance of the odour that emanates from poorly maintained systems. To an engineer, this problem seems facile since there are ways to manage odour. However, this has proven to be a significant barrier to a more widespread adoption of GW management solutions.

Perhaps the most significant conclusion is that the failure of most GW treatment and use systems can be directly linked with an overemphasis on technical solutions that misunderstand local cultural and social realities. This is emphatically illustrated by the fact that while GW management systems seem to have more economic benefits in comparison to cesspits, they remain less popular with the public. The suggestion here is that there is a major need for mobilizing education and training will be fundamental to any further work on the subject in MENA (Abu-Madi et al., Chapter 6 this volume).

Conclusion

With all of this knowledge in mind, the papers presented in this volume were discussed and reviewed in February 2007 at the Consultation on Greywater Use in Aqaba. One notable constraint is that much of the work to date is based on pilot projects that, while they illustrate useful approaches in community development, have produced only some research that does not always address the critical gaps. Papers are presented here that cover efforts to apply technical solutions to GW treatment and management, how technology is developed and used, as well as social and cultural acceptance of GW use. Also, as noted earlier, this work focuses on the application of household GW for irrigation in rural areas. Other uses, such as for toilet flushing, landscape irrigation, or use in an urban context are not addressed here.

Notes

1   A joint project of WHO, IDRC, and FAO is pilot testing low-cost approaches to conducting health-risk analysis, developing health-based targets in difficult contexts, and also piloting innovative solutions to reduce risk. The project is taking place at two sites in Ghana, one site in Senegal, and one in Jordan whose main focus is GW.

References

Al-Damkhi, A.M. (2008) 'Environmental ethics in Islam: Principles, violations and future perspectives', *The International Journal of Environmental Studies* 65(1): 11–31.

Armitage, N.P., Winter, K., Spiegel, A. and Kruger, E. (2009) 'Community-focused greywater management in two informal settlements in South Africa', *Water Science & Technology* 59 (12): 2341–2350.

Ashour, J. and Jamrah, A. (2008) 'Survival of bacteria in soil subsequent to greywater application', *The International Journal of Environmental Studies* 65: 51–6.

Carden, K., Armitage, N., Winter, K., Sichone, O., Rivett, U. and Kahonde, J. (2005) 'The use and disposal of greywater in the non-sewered areas of South Africa (1): quantifying the greywater generated and assessing its quality', *Water South Africa* 33: 425–32.

Casanova, L.M., Little, V., Frye, R.J. and Gerba, C.P. (2001) 'A survey of the microbiological quality of household graywater', *Journal of American Water Resources Association* 37: 1313–19.

Department of Statistics (DOS) (2001) *Jordan in Figures*. Hashemite Kingdom of Jordan, Issue 4.

Faruqui, N. and Bino M. (2001) *Water management in Islam*, United Nations Press, Tokyo.

Friedler, E. (2008) 'The water saving potential and the socio-economic feasibility of greywater use within the urban sector – Israel as a case study', *The International Journal of Environmental Studies* 65: 57–70.

Gross, A., Wiel-Shafran, A., Bondarenko, N. and Ronen, Z. (2008) 'Reliability of small scale greywater treatment systems and the impact of its effluent on soil properties', *The International Journal of Environmental Studies* 65: 41–50.

Gross, A., Azulai, N., Oron, G., Ronen, Z., Arnold, M. and Nejidat A. (2005) 'Environmental impact and health risks associated with greywater irrigation: a case study', *Water Science and Technology* 52: 161–9.

Homer-Dixon, T. (1994) 'Environmental scarcities and violent conflict: evidence from cases', *International Security* 19: 5–40.

International Development Research Centre (IDRC) (2009) *Water Demand Initiative for the Middle East and North Africa (WaDImena)* [online], available from: http://www.idrc.ca/waterdemand [accessed 15 January 2009].

IWA Specialist Group (2000) 'Constructed wetlands for pollution control: processes, performance, design, operation', *Scientific and Technical Report No. 8*, IWA Publishing, London.

Lens, P., Zeeman, G. and Lettinga, G. (2001) 'Decentralized sanitation and reuse: concepts, systems and implementation', *Integrated Environmental Technology Series*, IWA Publishing, London.

Mara, D. and Cairncross, S. (1989) *Guidelines for the Safe Use of Wastewater and Excreta in Agriculture and Aquaculture*, World Health Organization, Geneva.

Mara, D. and Kramer A. (2008) 'The 2006 guidelines for wastewater and greywater use in agriculture: a practical interpretation', in I. Al Baz, R. Otterpohl, and C. Wendland (eds), *Efficient Management of Wastewater*, pp. 1–17, Springer, Amsterdam.

Memon, F.A., Butler, D., Han W., Liu, S., Makropoulos, C., Avery L.M. and Pidou, M. (2005) 'Economic assessment tool for greywater recycling systems', *Engineering Sustainability* 158: 155–61.

Noah, M. (2002) 'Graywater use is still a gray area', *Journal of Environmental Health* 64: 22–5.

Otterpohl, R. (2002) 'Options for alternative types of sewerage and treatment systems directed to the overall performance', *Water Science and Technology* 45: 149–58.

Pidou, M., Memon, F., Stephenson, T., Jefferson, B. and Jeffrey, P. (2007) 'Greywater recycling: treatment options and applications', *Engineering Sustainability* 160: 119–31.

Redwood, M. (2008a) 'The application of pilot research on greywater in the Middle East North Africa Region (MENA)', *The International Journal of Environmental Studies* 65: 109–18.

Redwood, M. (2008b) *Greywater irrigation: challenges and opportunities* in CAB Reviews: Perspectives in Agriculture, Veterinary Science, Nutrition and Natural Resources 2008 3, No. 063, London: CAB International 2008.

Stenekes, N., Colebatch, H., Waite, D. and Ashbolt, N. (2006) 'Risk and governance in water recycling: public acceptance revisited', *Science, Technology and Human Values* 31: 107–34.

Swiss Federal Institute of Aquatic Science and Technology (EAWAG) (2006) *Greywater Management in Low and Middle-Income Countries*, EAWAG, Dubendorf.

UN-Habitat (2008) *The State of African Cities Report*. UN-Habitat, Nairobi.

Wiel-Shafran, A., Ronen, Z., Weisbrod, N., Adar, E. and Gross, A. (2006) 'Potential changes in soil properties following irrigation with surfactant-rich greywater', *Ecological Engineering* 26: 348–54.

World Bank (2008) 'Brief: water management in MENA region' [online], available from: http://www.worldbank.org [accessed 15 December 2008].

World Health Organisation (WHO) (2006) *Guidelines for the Safe Use of Wastewater, Excreta and Greywater* (vols 1–4), WHO, Geneva.

WHO (2008) *Using Human Waste Safely for Livelihoods, Food Production and Health: Information Kit on the 3rd Edition of the Guidelines for the Safe Use of Wastewater, Excreta and Greywater in Agriculture and Aquaculture*, WHO, Food and Agriculture Organization of the United Nations (FAO), IDRC and International Water Management Institute (IWMI) [online], available from: http://www.who.int/water_sanitation_health/wastewater/usinghuman-waste/en/index.html [accessed 12 May 2009].

About the author

Mark Redwood is the programme leader for the Urban Poverty and Environment (UPE) initiative at IDRC. He is a specialist on environmental issues with a specific focus on urban water management and urban agriculture. Since 2002, he has developed and managed IDRC projects related to urban agriculture and wastewater recycling. His regions of work included Sub-Saharan Africa, the Middle East, and North Africa. He holds a Master's in Urban Planning from McGill University and has contributed to numerous publications, conferences, and peer-review journals. Email: mredwood@idrc.ca

PART I

Technical aspects

CHAPTER 2

On-site greywater treatment in Qebia Village, Palestine

Jamal Burnat and Intissar Eshtayah

*Qebia is one of the poorest villages of the western Ramallah area. It has a popu-
lation of 6,500 and is characterized by high unemployment especially among
men. A survey conducted in the Qebia area showed that 43 per cent of families
have more than 10 children, and 49 per cent have an average income of less than
US$300 per month. Greywater forms about 80 per cent of the total wastewater
produced at the household level, and it is demonstrated that at least 60 per cent
can be recovered, treated, and used, producing at least 150,000 litres of treated
GW per household per year. The aim of this chapter is to assess the impact of GW
systems on the environment, health, and socioeconomic factors at the household
level, by using water and soil sampling, as well as the results from a questionnaire
distributed to 48 beneficiary households of one GW treatment project.*

Introduction

Water scarcity is one of the most difficult problems facing the Palestinian
Territories. The lack of water resources and competition between different
uses – domestic, agricultural and industrial – is increasing year on year. The
pollution of water resources is also restricting the availability of water – the
wastewater cesspits used by Palestinians are a source of groundwater pollution. The high water usage, as well as disposal of wastewater from Israeli
settlements in the West Bank, is also cited as contaminating the soil and
further reducing the water resources available for Palestinians. Despite, or
perhaps because of, this scarcity, some families estimate that 20 per cent of
their monthly income is used on water and wastewater management.

A typical Palestinian family of 7 consumes an average of 350 litres of water
per day with limited access to disposal facilities. Many families empty their
household wastewater into a 30 m³ cesspit. Typical monthly wastewater production is 14.7 m³ (80 per cent GW) which fills the average cesspit in less than
three months, forcing families to empty their cesspits four times per year. The
majority of families (88 per cent) empty cesspits into mobile tankers at a cost
of US$22 per month. Most of the remainder do not pay at all for the emptying
of cesspits. This leads to typical yearly expenditures for cesspit management
of around US$270. This represents 5 per cent of the household income for a

family with an average annual household income of US$5,500. When combined with the expense of maintaining the cesspits and freshwater expenditures, more than 10 per cent of the average family's annual household income can be spent on water purchases and wastewater management.

In the village of Qebia, families (like many others in Palestine) spend a significant proportion of their income on water purchased for domestic and agricultural purposes. Most families purchase at least 300 m³ of water per year at a minimum cost of US$1/m³, spending at least US$300 annually on freshwater. Some families have access to conventional water-harvesting sources such as cisterns. In these cases, perhaps 75 m³ of harvested rainwater can be stored per cistern and used for both domestic and agricultural uses.

The Qebia Women's Cooperative (QWC) was established in Qebia village in 2004 to serve the women of the village. The Cooperative aims to improve the social and economic status of women in the village through providing training and education. The Cooperative has provided training in: 1) food processing; 2) production and marketing of home made products; 3) social and educational issues such as family planning. The Cooperative also has facilitated a saving and credit programme to help women access funding resources for small projects.

Between September 2005 and June 2006, the QWC implemented a GW treatment-and-use project, serving 48 families and treating about 0.5 m³ per day per family. The treated GW was used for irrigating home gardens, mostly consisting of fruit trees and vegetables to be cooked and eaten. These installations were funded by Agricultural Cooperative Development International and Volunteers in Overseas Cooperative Assistance (ACDI-VOCA) to encourage the use of treated GW in agriculture to improve food security.

The overall objective of the project was to assess the impact of GW systems on the environment, health and socioeconomic issues at the household level. Contributing goals included:

- standardizing the existing on-site treatment plant design;
- assessing the effectiveness of the system on the wider community;
- assessing, monitoring and evaluating the performance of the pilot GW treatment and use systems;
- preparing capital, and operation- and maintenance-cost figures for the water management system at the household level;
- assessing the development of water resources for agricultural purposes by increasing the amount of water available through effective GW recovery, treatment, and use;
- assessing the establishment of an optimal process for household agricultural domestic GW use;
- assessing the promotion of community involvement concerning the issues of wastewater treatment and use;
- promoting the involvement of local community, children and youth, regional institutions, and policy makers in the appropriate and cost-effective community wastewater management and awareness schemes.

This chapter describes the project, measures the environmental and socio-economic impacts of the GW use through the project life, and provides an assessment of the situation before and after the implementation of the project.

Methodology

Questionnaire

A questionnaire was formulated to identify the hazards related to using fresh GW, the risks to the environment and effects on agriculture. The questionnaire was distributed to the 48 families in Qebia who benefited from greywater treatment (GWT) units as part of the project. Forty-seven completed surveys were received, noting that two families benefited from one shared treatment unit. The questionnaire covered the environment, health and socioeconomic situation in the household, before and after the installation of the GWT units. Statistical analysis was carried out using the SPSS program and standard analysis methodology.

Household pilot plant model and water analysis

The type of GWT unit was chosen following an intensive literature survey and reports from other field investigations. Available on-site treatment systems were analysed and evaluated with regard to design, performance, operation and maintenance, environmental impact (air pollution, noise production, soil pollution and ground water pollution), energy consumption and construction and operation cost. The system chosen for this project was a septic tank, up-flow gravel filter system, designed to treat GW produced from households sized from 6 to 25 inhabitants. The up-flow gravel filter is designed as a gravity-loaded system, with a maximum flow during the day and zero flow at night. The main treatment stage is an anaerobic process, which is followed by an aerobic multilayered filter containing sand, coal, and gravel. The unit requires that the household plumbing separates GW from toilet wastewater. Toilet wastewater is discharged to the existing or modified cesspit, while GW is directed to the treatment plant.

The layout of the pilot plant is shown in Figure 2.1. The gravel filter medium is mostly a crushed, hard limestone, 0.7–3.0 cm in size. The tanks are made of concrete and/or bricks, and are divided into four compartments. The first compartment is a septic tank and grease trap and receives the GW – from the shower, kitchen, sinks and washing machine – through a 5 or 7.5 cm diameter PVC pipe, via a screened manhole, by means of a T-shaped outlet. One end of this outlet is directed upward and open to atmospheric pressure and the other is at a level of about 30 cm from the bottom of the tank. The second and third tanks act as up-flow graduated gravel filters. The fourth compartment acts as a balancing tank for the treated GW, with a submersible pump installed to lift the water to a multilayered aerobic filter. Through a controlled flow from the top tank, the GW passes through the filter layers (sand, coal, and gravel – as shown in Figure 2.2) to a storage tank from where it can then be supplied to the irrigation network.

The retention time of the wastewater in the first tank (septic tank) is 1.5–2 days. Any accumulated grease is prevented from continuing through the system by the T-shape pipe, with GW taken from a depth far enough below the surface (to avoid taking in accumulated grease) and above the base of the tank (to avoid settled solids from being taken in).

The up-flow gravel filter design (tanks 2 and 3) is based on a void space of 40 per cent in tank 2 and 50 per cent in tank 3, with a design organic loading of

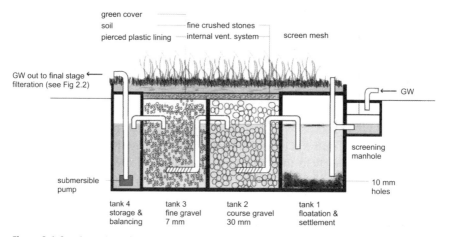

Figure 2.1 Septic tank up-flow gravel filter treatment unit

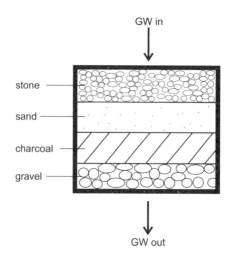

Figure 2.2 Final stage greywater filtration

Table 2.1 Methods of analysis

Item	Method
Chemical oxygen demand (COD)	Closed reflux, calorimetric method, spectrophotometer
Biochemical oxygen demand (BOD)	Standard method
Ammonia (NH3)	Direct nesslerization method
Kjeldahl nitrogen (NKj)	Macro-Kjeldahl method
Phosphate (p)	Ascorbic acid spectrophotometric method
Chloride (Cl)	Argontometric titration method
Sulfate (SO4)	Tubiditmetric method
Nitrate (NO3)	Photometric method

0.388 kg BOD/day, typical for a 10-person household. The hydraulic retention time is 2 days for the septic tank and 1.8 days for the up-flow gravel filter.

Water samples from the treatment units were collected and analysed using standard methods, by the Palestinian Water Authority Laboratory. Laboratory tests were done on 30 samples. Sample results were tested in triplicate. The storage and analysis of samples followed the Standard Methods for the Examination of Water and Wastewater (APHA et al., 1995). Table 2.1 summarizes the analysis methodology.

Results

From the questionnaire

Qebia village has 6,500 inhabitants, with a high percentage of unemployment. The survey reported that 50 per cent of households have an income of less than US$400 per month and an average water consumption of 50 litres per capita per day for domestic uses.

The survey found that most people in the study area were already using untreated GW for irrigation. In the study area, most houses have a garden which is used to cultivate a small amount of fruit and vegetables for consumption. Of the 48 households surveyed, only 2 had less than 500 m² of available ground, while 20 had between 1,000 and 2,000 m². On average, 55.5 per cent of the available land is cultivated with fruit trees and vegetables and the remainder is left uncultivated because of lack of water, the poor economic situation, or the quality of the land.

Householders pay US$1.2/m³ for piped water. Water at this rate is considered too expensive for small garden agriculture by poor families, especially those who are headed by women. This led more than 90 per cent of the villagers to separate their household GW and use it without treatment in the gardens, with the toilet wastewater directed to the cesspit.

Women were shown to play an important role in both food and water management in the project area. In 47 per cent of the households, only women were involved in food production by irrigation with GW, compared to 9 per cent households where only men were involved. Men, women, and/or children were together involved in garden irrigation in 44 per cent of households.

Many households noted problems caused by odours, insects and clogging of the pipes and the soil, from the use of untreated GW. Untreated greywater was reported to clog the soil void spaces, preventing ventilation and drainage and encouraging the growth of algae and fungi (Figure 2.3). Offensive odours were often noted, both around the houses and in the wider neighbourhoods – 36 per cent of the neighbours of GW users were reported to suffer from flies, mosquitoes and insects, which were attributed to GW use.

According to the survey, although 89 per cent of households use untreated GW in irrigating their home gardens, and most of the products go to family consumption, 53 per cent believe that untreated GW has a negative impact on the soil and plants, but use it nevertheless, both to reduce the cost of emptying the cesspit and to increase the water available for irrigation.

The use of untreated GW in agriculture is often a suspected cause of health problems. The survey showed that 57 per cent of the families who used untreated GW reported themselves to be infected by amoebae (42 per cent), psoriasis (8 per cent), or both (8 per cent). A high majority (94 per cent) reported that they use pesticides for mosquito control, but 79 per cent believed that these pesticides were insufficient to combat mosquitoes breeding on GW seepage. Mosquito control can cost more than US$100 per summer season, and 81 per cent of respondents believed that pesticides had a negative affect on the family health.

Figure 2.3 Fresh greywater polluting home garden soil

Disposal of the remaining wastewater is also problematic. After leaving the households, the mobile tankers, containing the contents of the emptied cesspits, usually dispose of the wastewater in nearby open areas and valleys. This seriously pollutes the quality of soil and the surface and groundwater resources and is suspected of causing knock-on health problems. According to the survey, costs for medical treatment of water-borne diseases ranges from US$50 to US$500 per family per year, although this cannot be directly attributed to pollution from wastewater disposal.

Following the installation and use of the GWT units, the survey was used to examine changes in perceptions. Sixty per cent of respondents reported that the treatment units had a positive impact on reducing the cost of mosquito control, increasing the availability of irrigation water leading to an increase in cultivated area. Forty-nine per cent of the households believed that irrigating with treated wastewater improved the growth of the plants. Respondents also reported an improvement in social relationships with neighbours, due to reduced odours and the lower frequency of cesspit emptying.

From greywater analysis

Table 2.2 shows the range of results from water quality testing of 30 triplicate samples of GW before and after treatment in the units. Untreated GW in Qebia was found to be heavily polluted with bio-degradable matter, with COD levels varying from 1,390 to 2,400 mg/l, and therefore requiring treatment before use. The efficiency of the installed treatment systems was high, reducing COD levels to 58–266 mg/l, levels which meet the WHO standards for GW use. The faecal coliform counts were reduced by two orders of magnitude, from a range of $1–37\times10^4$ to $0–1\times10^2$ cfu/100 ml.

Table 2.2 Characteristics of untreated greywater from the Qebia Project

Parameter	Unit	GW influent	GW effluent	WHO/FAO guidelines
DO	mg/l	0	0.5–2.0	
pH		6.60–6.86	6.70–7.79	6.5–8.4[b]
BOD	mg/l	941–997	21–121	20[c]
COD	mg/l	1,391–2,405	58–266	
NH_4^+-N	mg/l	25–45	12–48	
Surfactant		11–17	5–13	
NO_3^-	mg/l	0–1.3	13–36	9.5–518.5[b]
Total Suspended Solids (TSS)	mg/l	36–396	4–24	20[c]
EC		891–899	844–1,493	0.7–3.0 (dS/m)[b]
Total Dissolved Solids (TDS)	mg/l	483–515	465–849	450–2,000[b]
Faecal coliforms	cfu/100 ml	$1\times10^4–37\times10^4$	$0–1\times10^2$	200[a]
Total coliforms	cfu/100 ml	$1\times10^9–5\times10^9$	$2\times10^2–10\times10^2$	1,000[c]

a WHO 1989 guidelines for public parks and crops likely to be eaten uncooked
b FAO guideline for water quality for irrigation
c WHO/AFESD Consultation, limit for vegetables likely to be eaten uncooked

These results show that the GW before treatment is polluted to the extent that it is not acceptable for use on home gardens, according to the WHO guidelines. The treatment process adequately reduces the concentration of organic pollutants and faecal coliforms to within acceptable limits for fruit trees and vegetables to be cooked and eaten. However, the levels of BOD, faecal coliforms and nitrates in some cases are in exceedance of the guidelines for vegetables to be eaten raw.

Regarding the bacterial sampling, the total coliform group includes four genera in the Enterobacteriaceae family – *Escherichia*, *Klebsiella*, *Citrobacter*, and *Enterobacter*. Of the group, the *Escherichia* genus (*E. coli*) is taken as representative of faecal contamination. The faecal coliforms in the post-treatment samples show concentrations between 0 and 1×10^2 cfu/100 ml. The higher results occurred in houses with small children who are bathed in sinks. The Palestinian Department for Standards and Measurements Guidelines allow for faecal coliforms to reach 1,000 cfu/100 ml for unrestricted agriculture.

Results from this project indicate that there should be a significant reduction in environmental impact from treated GW. One immediately noticeable reported effect was a reduction in soil pollution and a reduction of odours, as well as a more pleasing visual environment in the irrigated areas.

Discussion and conclusion

Observations and tests carried out on the GWT units during the project have allowed improvements and refinements to be made, which addressed some of the problems observed during operation. The treatment was able to be standardized to its current form – a septic tank followed by up-flow anaerobic gravel filter with two compartments of different grain size, followed by a storage and balancing tank with a submersible pump to lift the treated water to a multilayer aerobic filter. The dimensions of the treatment plant were also standardized according to three family size distributions in the area – with up to 10, 15, and 20 persons per household. Detailed drawings were prepared for these three different sizes of treatment plants.

Improvements were also made to the drip irrigation. All of the home gardens have drip irrigation networks. Both past experience and the literature showed that drip irrigation is an optimal way to use water. However for treated GW, flushed material can clog the drippers. Thus, a water filter was installed to protect the drippers from clogging. This filter has to be maintained regularly.

It was observed that the GWT units address some of the problems of using untreated wastewater. The units allow families access to an innovative source of water. Greywater generated at the household level is easily and efficiently treated in typical amounts of 130 m³ per household annually. The water is treated using natural methods, with very low energy consumption, in units that are easy to operate and maintain. Stage I of the project saw 23 of these GWT and use systems installed and operating. After receiving requests from others, QWC installed 25 more systems, based on an up-flow anaerobic filter followed by an aerobic filter. Water bills were reduced and expenditures on pumping out the cesspit also reduced dramatically. Beneficiaries maintain their systems, since they obtained a direct benefit from them. The treatment technology is simple and low cost. The required materials are locally available, and there is no need for skilled personnel to operate and maintain them. Other operation and maintenance costs, including energy consumption costs, are low, at around US$20 per year, and the effluent is of adequate quality to be used.

From this positive experience, it is expected that the beneficiaries in Qebia will encourage other community members to invest in these units for their own households.

The 30 laboratory tests carried out on the water quality and treatment plant performance and GW characteristics showed it to be suitable for agricultural use. Since the treated GW is being used for agriculture, purchased water can be either saved or reallocated to other uses. The treated GW can only be used for agriculture, but enough can be generated to irrigate between 100 and 200 m^2 of greenhouse crops or 500 m^2 of open-field home gardens. Using GWT to irrigate greenhouses can also help to ensure a continuous supply of water and food production, and QWC is planning to consider supplementary projects in the future. Greywater is a stable source of water, contains natural fertilizers and is 'free of charge'. After installing and operating the wastewater management systems, the GW is treated and used, while the remaining (roughly 20 per cent) of wastewater (blackwater) goes to a modified cesspit, where it is treated and disposed of in the usual way. This increased efficiency of water usage increased the positive public perception of the units.

According to the survey, only 36 per cent of the households believed that using untreated GW affects health. The project therefore included an awareness programme, which highlighted to villagers, including school children, the risks of the use of untreated GW and the benefits of GWT. The treatment units were explained, and comparisons made between the situation before and after installation. Villagers (both men and women) were also involved in a training and extension programme. The beneficiaries also contributed to the construction of the treatment and irrigation systems, were active in solving on-site work problems and seemed happy to follow the directions of QWC on operating the system and reusing the treated greywater. QWC contributed to the needs assessment, planning, the beneficiary selection, tendering, and administrative as well as financial follow-up of the project. Local women's co-operatives from neighbouring communities and local, as well as, international NGOs visited the project site to observe the programme.

In addition to the positive economic impact of GW use, the project has positively impacted women on two levels. First, since in most households the woman is responsible for water and cesspit management, being able to use GW reduces the amount of time spent on water management, allowing women to pay more attention to their families and gardens. Second, since the late arrival of pump trucks often causes cesspits to overflow and strain relationships with neighbours, reducing the load on the cesspits is an advantage of the GW use project.

Recommendations

The Palestinian people are suffering from a number of acute problems that need immediate alleviation, not simply further studies. Problems which need investment are often beyond the capacity of local people to solve alone. Through this project in the Qebia village, a practical impact has been seen. The key advantages of GWT in this area were seen to be twofold. It has provided additional water volumes that can be used for developing agriculture and improving the food security for the Qebia community. It has also reduced the pollution resulting from using untreated wastewater for irrigation, which leads to soil pollution with organic matter, pathogens and mosquitoes. It should be noted that the road blocks and travel restrictions imposed on the Palestinian territories by the Israeli military made monitoring of the systems in the field more time consuming.

In order to further alleviate the water shortages faced by Palestinians, and the environmental pollution arising from illegal discharge of wastewater, the following recommendations are made:

- Improve environmental awareness in the community, especially among young people in schools, colleges, and education centres.
- Establish more household GWT and use systems to reduce the negative environmental and social effects resulting from using untreated GW in agriculture.
- Encourage the use of non-conventional water sources in agriculture, via suitable irrigation systems.
- Intensify global research into GW recovery, treatment, and use studies to better examine the impacts on environment, socioeconomics and public health.

Acknowledgements

The authors present their deepest gratitude to QWC who have been implementing these projects, and ACDI-VOCA for their generous grant, which made it possible to implement and study this project. Special thanks go to the staff at the Palestinian Water Authority Laboratory, especially Mrs. Majeda Alawneh who took care of testing the samples.

Reference

American Public Health Association (APHA), American Water Works Association (AWWA) and Water Environment Federation (WEF) (1995) *Standard*

Methods for the Examination of Water and Wastewater, 19th edn APHA, Washington D.C.

About the authors

Jamal Burnat is a water and environmental sanitation specialist in a food security programme at ACDI-VOCA. He is a water and environment engineer with experience in on-site wastewater management systems. He is also the developer of the controlled up-flow gravel filter for on-site grey wastewater treatment and reuse. He holds an MSc. degree in Low Cost Water Supply and Environmental Sanitation Management from IHE, Delft, the Netherlands. Email: jburnat@gmail.com

Intissar Eshtayah is an agronomist & community development specialist who worked at ACDIVOCA on gender and community development issues.

CHAPTER 3

Greywater use in rural home gardens in Karak, Jordan

Murad Bino, Shihab Al Beiruti and Mohammad Ayesh

The Karak project was conducted in the Karak Governorate in southern Jordan between February 2004 and October 2007, with the aim of helping the peri-urban poor benefit from the use of treated GW in their home gardens. This chapter will describe the benefits and the concerns related to GW use. Two simple and low-cost GW treatment (GWT) units – the four barrel and the confined trench type – were installed in 110 low-income households not served by a sewerage network. The resulting GW was used to irrigate crops that are not eaten raw. The quality of treated GW obtained by these units was shown to be in accordance with both Jordanian and WHO guidelines for the use of treated wastewater.

This use of treated GW resulted in savings of potable water supplied to the households and in minimizing the frequency of emptying of the households' cesspits. On average, it was possible to recover up to 237 litres of treated GW daily, for a family of eight. This quantity was sufficient to provide the daily supplementary irrigation needs of about 25 olive trees, as well as other garden crops and forages. Overall, despite concerns, the monitoring impacts of GW use on plants indicated no bacteriological contamination. The treated GW use was well accepted by the community in the project area, and many considered their GWT units to be valued household possessions.

Background

Many countries in the arid and semi-arid parts of the Middle East and North Africa (MENA) region are facing a continuing decline of per capita water availability due to high population growth rates, improved living standards and industrialization. Jordan is among the most water-scarce countries in the region and has made significant achievements over the past two decades in restructuring its water sector and adopting a clear water strategy. This water strategy identified wastewater as a resource that has to be treated and used effectively while safeguarding public health and the environment. Jordan is also among the first countries of the region to ration domestic water-supply and place tariffs on the consumption of irrigation water. According to Water

Authority data, a sewerage network covers 60 per cent of Jordan's urban areas and nearly all treated sewage is used for irrigation (WAJ, 2005). Towns and villages in rural areas not covered with sewerage networks use cesspits or septic tanks. The emptying of cesspits in some parts of Jordan has become a source of pollution to groundwater and a costly practice for the poor.

As a result of insufficient domestic-water supplies in some countries like Jordan, Palestine, Lebanon, and Yemen, household GW is often used, treated or untreated for the irrigation of home gardens (Burnat and Eshtayah, Chapter 2 this volume; CSBE, 2003; Haddad El-Hajj, Chapter 9 this volume). Greywater is composed of varied quantities of components of wastewater that may come from the shower, bath, hand basin, laundry and kitchen sink. Greywater, therefore, is comprised of those components of sewage that does not come from a toilet or urinal. Greywater contains impurities and micro-organisms derived from household and personal cleaning activities. While bathroom and laundry water are relatively benign, kitchen water often deserves special attention since it is loaded with organic matter from food wastes. Greywater is distinct from blackwater (from the toilet or urinal) as there are fewer health and environmental risks associated with its use. If used wisely and appropriately, GW – including its separation, containment and use – can be a simple home-based water-demand management strategy that has benefits at the household level as it can be considered as an alternative water resource to optimize productivity (Redwood, 2007). It is estimated that 55–60 per cent of rural household wastewater effluent is GW (INWRDAM, 2007).

The International Development Research Centre (IDRC) conducted a workshop in Gaza with the Palestinian Agricultural Relief Committees (PARC) that examined priority research-needs related to urban agriculture in MENA countries. Workshop participants concluded that GW use was a very promising research area. IDRC decided to develop a number of projects related to urban agriculture and GW use. This chapter discusses one such project.

Project description

Phase I: Tafila

IDRC advanced a grant to the Inter-Islamic Network on Water Resources Development and Management, Amman, Jordan (INWRDAM) to conduct the Tafila Greywater Treatment and Use for Poverty Reduction project in Jordan during 2000–2003 (the Tafila project).

The Tafila project focused on investigating and improving a number of on-site GWT methods that could be suitable for treating GW from peri-urban low-income households and assuring that the quality of effluent would be suitable for irrigating garden crops. The Tafila project was implemented in the town of Ein Al-Baida in the Tafila Governorate in southern Jordan. The main mosque, 22 houses and a girls' secondary school in Ein Al- Baida were fitted with various types of GWT units. Five different GWT methods were investigated in the Tafila project, from which two methods: the four-barrel method and the confined trench (CT) GW treatment method were selected as likely candidates for further refinement and scaling-up (see below). The Tafila project recommended that GWT methods targeted at the low-income rural poor must be inexpensive to construct, require low running and operation costs, and must be capable of producing effluents that meet the restricted irrigation guidelines (for the irrigation of crops not eaten raw) of the World Health Organization (WHO, 2006) and the Jordanian Standard No. 893/2006 – Effluent Grade C (JISM, 2006).

In 2002, the Ministry of Planning of Jordan initiated a national programme aiming at improving the social and economic productivity of the poor in Jordan. On February 2002, the Ministry of Planning contracted INWRDAM to implement 689 GWT units of the four-barrel type in 91 rural villages in Jordan. This was a clear sign that the government of Jordan considered GW use as a means for alleviating poverty and conserving freshwater.

In 2004, IDRC contracted PLAN:NET Ltd (P:N), a Canadian development consulting company, to conduct a detailed post-project evaluation of 50 GWT units implemented by INWRDAM in Jordan, including the Tafila project. The post-project evaluation conducted by P:N resulted in a set of main recommendations and concluded that GW systems implemented by INWRDAM were technically effective, but that more attention should be given to the socio-economic dimensions and the long-term impacts of GW use on soil if future and wider applications of GWT systems were to be planned (PLAN:NET, 2004). This is discussed further by Keough and his colleagues in this volume.

Domestic water consumption and GW disposal from five households of eight family members in the Tafila project were monitored between 2001 and 2003. On average, 57 per cent of household wastewater can be recovered as GW (INWRDAM, 2003). This value is comparable with values estimated by other researchers, such as Redwood (2007) who reported that the proportion of household wastewater that is GW varies from 65 to 80 per cent. Based on the positive outcomes of the Tafila project, IDRC decided on February 2004 to provide INWRDAM with a research grant to implement another GW project in a suitable location in Jordan.

Selection of greywater treatment unit type

Between 2001 and 2005, INWRDAM developed and tested five different GWT units. Figures 3.1–3.5 show views of the different types of GWT units developed and tested by INWRDAM.

The two types chosen for further improvement and scale-up are discussed below. The first type was a four-barrel unit and can treat up to 200 litres of GW per day. The other unit was known as the CT and can treat up to 300 litres of GW per day. Both units can produce GW effluents suitable for restricted irrigation.

Figure 3.1 Two-barrel greywater treatment unit

Figure 3.2 Four-barrel greywater treatment unit

Figure 3.3 Confined trench greywater treatment unit

Figure 3.4 Circular concrete greywater treatment unit

Figure 3.5 Rectangular concrete greywater treatment unit

A standard four-barrel GWT unit consists of four recycled polyethylene (PE) plastic barrels connected together by polyvinyl chloride (PVC) pipes. Figure 3.6 shows construction details of a standard four-barrel GWT unit.

Pre-treatment takes place in a 50-litre barrel where grease, oil and settled solids are removed by filtration and gravity effects. A bag filter made of 0.5 mm polyester net is inserted on the feed pipe. The bag filter captures food and other solid particles originating from the kitchen sink, and soil, hair, and lint from washing clothes and other household water. The bag filter helps reduce the suspended solid content of the GW. Filtered GW then passes from the

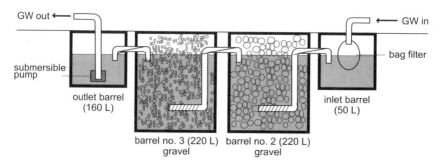

Figure 3.6 Four-barrel treatment unit

first barrel into the second and third PE barrels, each of which had a capacity of 220 litres. The second and third barrels were filled with gravel 2–3 cm in diameter, which acts as a submerged gravel medium maintained under anaerobic conditions. Flow in the second and third barrels is directed in such a way that GW passes in an up-flow direction through the gravel medium so as to achieve biological treatment over a retention time of two to three days. The fourth PE barrel has a capacity of 160 litres and is fitted with a small electric pump, which delivers treated GW to a trickle irrigation system serving a small garden of trees. Regular cleaning of the first barrel in which pre-treatment of GW took place was found necessary to prevent the emission of odours and clogging of the gravel media in the second and third barrels. Except for the regular cleaning of the bag filter and inspection and alignment of the pump, the maintenance of the four-barrel unit is minimal. The cost of materials and installation of the four-barrel unit was estimated at US$261 based on 2006 prices. More details on the quality of treated GW and the economic feasibility of the four-barrel unit are provided later in this chapter.

The CT unit is a modification of the four-barrel unit and can treat larger quantities of GW effectively. This modification was accomplished by replacing the second and third barrels in the four-barrel unit with a dug trench lined with impermeable plastic sheeting about 400 micron thick and filled with 3 m³ of gravel medium 2–3 cm in size. Figure 3.7 shows construction details of the CT unit.

Treated GW from the CT unit was pumped automatically through a trickle irrigation system to a small home garden. The cost of construction of a standard CT unit is estimated at US$300 based on 2006 prices and could treat up to 300 litres of GW per day.

Phase II: The Karak project – introduction, location, and objectives

INWRDAM and PLAN:NET together developed the criteria that specify community and site characteristics necessary for GW use practices (PLAN:NET, 2004). These include the following:

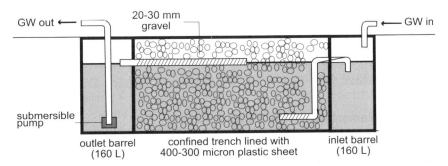

Figure 3.7 Confined trench treatment unit

- peri-urban community;
- presence of governmental and community organizations;
- sufficient number of low-income households with home gardens;
- arable soil and moderate rainfall (minimum 200 mm/year);
- not served by public sewers and unlikely to be served in the near future;
- need for water – no easy access to natural water sources, such as springs, wells, and irrigation canals.

Different rural areas in Jordan were considered, based on the results of the Tafila project, in order to identify a suitable location for a scaled-up project. The Al-Amer villages of Abu-Trabah, Masa'ar, Mugayer, Ariha, and Al-Alia, and a second nearby community in the Village of Al-Jada'a in the Governorate of Karak met the selection criteria mentioned above. These villages constitute a cluster of peri-urban settlements located 45 km from the centre of Karak Governorate and spread over an area of about 17 km². The total population of these villages in 2004 was approximately 8,000 concentrated mainly in Al-Jada'a Village. This peri-urban area was not served with sewer networks and all households used cesspits. All houses were connected to electricity and domestic water-supply networks. Due to the unreliable nature of the domestic water-supply, some families had to purchase water from tankers at the high price of around US$2.5/m³. The majority of the houses included in the project were modest and surrounded by a garden traditionally planted with olive trees. Greywater could be separated from blackwater and used without much alteration of the premises.

IDRC agreed on February 2004 to provide INWRDAM with a grant to conduct the Karak project with the following objectives:

- To expand and scale up the number of GW treatment and use units to serve a peri-urban community.
- To enhance the design and construction of the GW systems so as to attain the best possible GW effluent quantity and quality, reducing odour and long-term environmental impacts.
- To monitor social, environmental and economic impacts of GW use.
- To establish, maintain, and monitor household productive gardens with the aim of increasing household income and understanding the long-term impact of GW use on soils and crops.
- To build local and national capacity and increase public participation to improve the operation and maintenance of the treatment systems and increase the likelihood of their adoption.

Project implementation – the Karak project

The Karak project location is characterized by severe water shortage and hot summers. The mean annual rainfall ranges from 200 to 250 mm, and domestic water-supply is rationed to a single day each week. The Al-Amer villages are situated at the end of a 30 km long domestic water-supply line, which results in low pressures in the domestic water-mains with only small amounts of water reaching consumers. Many families buy water from private vendors when domestic water-supplies run short in the summer months.

The Karak GW project team consisted of researchers in water treatment and wastewater quality, agriculture and the environment, and community development and socioeconomic analysis. The team also included a detergent specialist, engineers and local technicians. A local staff member from P:N participated in the community component of the project between February 2004 and February 2006. A project steering committee (SC) composed of representatives from the Jordanian ministries responsible for water, agriculture, social welfare, the environment, public health and planning was established to guide the project implementation and disseminate project results.

Setup – identification of area, households, and local stakeholder committee

At the early stages of the Karak project, the communities associated with the Al-Amer villages were informed about the project and its objectives. Field visits were held to local government offices in the project area to inform them about the project. Baseline data about the community was collected mainly through visits to local government offices and field surveys of households. During the first year of the project, 10 GW CT-type units were installed for demonstration and training purposes.

A local stakeholder committee (LSC) was formed of local stakeholders in the project area. A tentative list of potential beneficiaries was prepared based on the criteria of low income, monthly domestic water consumption, availability of garden area, ability to separate grey from blackwater, and the interest of the householders.

Professional trainers from previous INWRDAM GW projects were involved in installing the 10 demonstration GW units and in training a number of local technicians on the installation, operation and maintenance of GW units. A female technician was included in the training, in order to encourage female members of households to attend meetings and training sessions.

Initially, the Karak project considered that some cash or in-kind contribution should be required by the householders, in order for a household to be accepted for participation in the project. This would have increased the sense of ownership of beneficiaries for the GW units. However, this was not possible, mostly due to community reluctance to commit to a project whose direct benefits were as yet untested.

The target of the project was to construct 150 four-barrel and 150 CT units in the Al-Amer villages. However, it was possible to install only 110 GW units, mainly of the CT type, by the end of the project. The main reason for this was that many households were not ready, or able, to make the required in-kind or financial contribution in order to be accepted as a beneficiary of the project. The reluctance of households to make contributions to the project was partly due to the fact that most rewards accruing from GW use, i.e. higher garden yield and savings in the domestic water bill would be realized months after the installation of GW units.

Water quality monitoring

Analysis of the raw and treated GW was conducted to determine the chemical and bacteriological characteristics of the effluent, to find ways to conduct suitable training for the users of these units, and to assess the possible long-term impacts of GW on soil and plants. Sampling and analysis of GW was carried out during 2006 and 2007 at the laboratories of the Water Authority of Jordan, and soil and plant sampling was conducted by the National Centre for Agriculture Technology Transfer in Amman. Monitoring of GW commenced a year after commissioning, to allow sufficient time for the units to be running in a steady state condition. Greywater samples were collected at monthly intervals from December 2006 to September 2007. Soil and plant samples were collected at half-yearly intervals beginning in 2006.

Samples of raw GW flowing into the units were collected first by emptying and cleaning the first barrel of a treatment unit and allowing GW to collect over 24 hours. Collected raw water was stirred thoroughly before sampling. Treated GW was collected by emptying the barrel that received treated GW and allowing treated GW to flow into it overnight and then mixing the contents thoroughly before sampling. The results are discussed later.

Financial analysis

A financial and economic analysis was conducted to assess the socioeconomic feasibility of the Karak project. Two field surveys based on similar questionnaires were conducted, one during February 2005 by P:N and another during February 2006 by INWRDAM. The second field survey included 60 beneficiaries selected randomly, which made up about half of the total beneficiaries in the project area. The socioeconomic feasibility of the project was based on the outcome of a second survey conducted by INWRDAM at the stage when beneficiaries were better able to assess the benefits and costs of operating GW units. The results are discussed later.

Training on garden productivity

The Karak project investigated ways to increase home garden productivity and minimize the impact of GW on soil and plants. The typical area of an average household garden in the project was 1,500 m², planted usually with around 25 olive trees and some garden crops. Permaculture practices were introduced to the project community to help improve agricultural production and reduce possible long-term impacts of GW on soil and plants. Baseline properties of soil not subject to GW application were monitored by selecting two sites in the project area: one location at the Ariha Village that was closer to arid areas and with soils similar to Abu-Trabah and Al-Alia villages, and a second location at Al-Jada'a Village which was at a relatively higher elevation and with soils similar to the Masa'ar and Mugayer villages.

Olive trees are considered to be suitable plants for GW irrigation, as they can withstand drought and tolerate irrigation with domestic wastewater (see Burnat and Eshtayah, Chapter 2 in this volume). The Karak project introduced new garden crops that were not common in the area but were suitable for irrigation with GW. These new garden crops included: 1) fruit trees such as almonds and carob; 2) forages, e.g. Sudan grass, corn, millet, soya bean, fenugreek and mustard; 3) medical plants, mellissa and lavender; 4) legumes such as vetch, in addition to sweetcorn, sunflower, bean and Indian type okra. The local community was trained in the cultivation of these new crops.

Crops were planted in home gardens according to the available area. Different permaculture practices were introduced to the local community. Okra, corn, bean and sunflower were planted in rows under plastic mulching. Okra was intercropped with corn and sunflower at the same line to ensure plant diversity. Intercropping created a better local environment for okra during hot summer days and reduced the possibility of infection with disease. Other permaculture practices, such as soil organic mulching, on-site rain harvesting, composting of home garden waste, and planting legume crops, were implemented to increase soil organic matter, improve soil productivity and reduce the impact of GW on soil.

Manure was readily available in the project area since many of the beneficiary households raise animals. Solid compost was prepared from animal manure and plant residues and was used as a soil amendment in home gardens. Composting was carried out by an anaerobic method, by mixing manure with plant residues and straw in a ratio of one part manure to two parts plant residues. Tea compost, a solution of solid compost, was prepared from goat, chicken and pigeon manures by soaking and straining the solid compost through a thick cloth and mixing it with water in a ratio of 1 to 10 (1 kg of solid compost per 10 litres of water). This mixture was mixed daily over a period of 7–10 days.

Results and observations

Greywater quality

The quantity of treated GW generated from five representative units was measured. Measurements were conducted on a weekly basis over a period of six months. The average quantity of treated GW generated for a household of eight people was 237 litres/family/day. This is equivalent to 29.6 litres/person/day, almost half of the 59 litres/person/day average reported for Amman (Jamrah et al., 2006), and matches values reported by other researchers in Jordan (Halalsheh et al., 2008).

The water requirements of olive crops range from 400–600 mm/year. Jordan's Ministry of Agriculture recommends about 240 litres of irrigation water per olive tree in areas that receive rainfall of less than 400 mm a year. The critical water deficit period for an olive crop is during the hot summer months of July–September. The 240 litres correspond to 20 litres/tree/week. The GW amounts generated per household in the Karak project were found to be 237 litres per day, which was enough to provide supplementary irrigation for about 82 olive trees daily. This means that GW use could provide a home garden planted with 25 olive trees (INWRDAM, 2003) with all of the required supplementary irrigation water as well as extra water to irrigate other crops.

Table 3.1 shows the quality of raw GW obtained from five representative houses between December 2006 and March 2007. The allowable limits refer to the Jordanian Standard 893 or the 1989 WHO guidelines.

The results show that the raw GW quality varied over a wide range. The water was high in BOD_5 and COD values even when compared with total domestic sewage classifications recommended by wastewater treatment design textbooks (Metcalf and Eddy, 2003). This could be attributed to the fact that households used small amounts of water to discharge large quantities of pollutants, as in dish washing or washing clothes in single-tube washing machines. Also the GW units were small and the first barrel, which acted as a primary settling stage was of limited capacity necessitated by the need for easy

Table 3.1 Quality of raw greywater from representative houses

Main parameters of concern	pHunit	TSSmg/1	BODmg/1	CODmg/1
Allowable limit	6–9	150	300	500
Date of sampling: 18 December 2006				
SF House (CT)	Not tested	116	133	715
ANA House (CT)	Not tested	Not tested	Not tested	Not tested
MSA House (four-barrel)	5.93	358	528	1,497
MA House (four-barrel)	6.14	Not tested	528	3,330
OE House (CT)	7.02	Not tested	123	914
Date of sampling: 29 January 2007				
SF House (CT)	7.1	125	Not tested	1,019
ANA House (CT)	Not tested	Not tested	Not tested	Not tested
MSA House (four-barrel)	6.76	122	Not tested	546
MA House (four-barrel)	6.38	276	Not tested	830
OE House (CT)	7.24	23	Not tested	92
Date of sampling: 5 March 2007				
SA House (CT)	7.52	84	138	357
ANA House (CT)	6.12	214	1,240	2,263
MSA House (four-barrel)	7.36	111	180	344
MA House (four-barrel)	7.82	89	170	539
OE House (CT)	7.56	54	110	148
Average of three rounds of sampling	6.91	143	350	969
Range of values	5.93–7.82	23–358	110–1,240	92–3,330

cleaning. The low pH values mean that the first stage of treatment could be under septic conditions and could emit offensive odours if not cleaned often, as was observed by some beneficiaries. Odour reduction was achieved by training households to clean the GW units regularly.

Table 3.2 shows results of the treated GW obtained from typical CT and four-barrel units. The results show that these GW treatment units were able to treat variable quality GW to a quality suitable for restricted irrigation according to Jordanian and WHO guidelines for reclaimed wastewater use (WHO, 2006). An important observation was that the quality of effluent produced by the low cost four-barrel and CT units with regard to restricted irrigation use were comparable to those more expensive treatment units reported by other researchers (see Burnat and Eshtayah, Chapter 2 in this volume). Table 3.3 compares the ranges for both raw and treated GW.

Table 3.4 shows the results of an analysis of heavy metals in a sample of treated GW effluent. Heavy metals can be a problem when using GW in rural areas. As Table 3.4 shows, the concentration of heavy metals was well below allowable limits except for the concentration of chromium and nickel. The concentration of nickel was 10 times higher and that of chromium was 1.6 times higher than the allowable limits. In these cases, the source of nickel in wastewater was linked to the unregulated disposal of rechargeable batteries mainly from devices such as mobile phones. The fact that about 80 per cent of the population in Jordan use mobile phones could be a serious source of pollution with nickel and cadmium.

Impact on soil and plants

Some people in rural areas traditionally diverted the portion of GW coming from the kitchen into the garden without any treatment. Some people did so because of their belief that food – particles or liquid – should not be discharged to a cesspool (Halalsheh et al., 2008). Soil samples were collected and analysed once at the beginning and again at the end of the Karak project. Soil samples were collected from two depths: one represented surface soil up to a depth of 30 cm and the other represented deeper soils from a depth of 30–60 cm. Soil properties relating to the cultivation of olive trees and home garden crops were determined and included pH, electrical conductivity (EC), sodium adsorption ratio (SAR), percentage organic matter content (OM), calcium carbonate (CaCO$_3$), and soil texture.

Table 3.5 shows the results of the analysis of soil samples taken from locations not subject to GW irrigation. The salinity ranged from 0.34–0.62 dS/m. These results indicated that soils in the Ariha Village were less suitable for cultivation compared to soils in Al-Jada'a Village due to the high natural SAR ratio compared to the EC values (Gross et al., 2005). Natural soil properties in Ariha appeared to be more sodic than soils in Al-Jada'a as indicated by the higher SAR ratio. These soils were naturally enriched with CaCO$_3$ which was common for most Jordan calcareous soils. The percentage of organic matter

Table 3.2 Quality of treated greywater from four-barrel and CT units monitored between December 2006 and September 2007

Parameter	pH unit	TSS mg/1	BOD mg/1	COD mg/1	Nitratemg/1
Allowable limit	6–9	150	300	500	9
Date of sampling: 18 December 2006					
SF House (CT)	7.52	30	19	137	0.2
ANA House (CT)	6.96	116	141	1,196	0.2
MSA House (four-barrel)	7.19	94	131	739	0.51
MA House (four-barrel)	7.22	312	86	616	0.2
OE House (CT)	7.47	42	28	86	7.79
Date of sampling: 29 January 2007					
SF House (CT)	7.37	54	Not tested	394	0.2
ANA House (CT)	6.92	139	Not tested	1,828	Not tested
MSA House (four-barrel)	7.4	73	Not tested	204	0.2
MA House (four-barrel)	7.23	101	Not tested	471	0.2
OE House (CT)	7.6	25	Not tested	36	2.3
Date of sampling: 5 March 2007					
SF House (CT)	7.52	32	104	240	0.2
ANA House (CT)	7.47	214	914	2,020	0.43
MSA House (four-barrel)	7.62	98	92	215	0.21
MA House (four-barrel)	7.96	42	126	278	0.2
OE House (CT)	7.7	29	49	97	2.8
Date of sampling: 29 May 2007					
SF House (CT)	7.64	41	124	463	0.2
ANA House (CT)	7.33	226	783	2763	1.28
MSA House (four-barrel)	7.52	75	86	393	0.2
MA House (four-barrel)	7.48	33	106	175	0.28
OE House (CT)	7.81	12	10	68	0.42
Date of sampling: 20 June 2007					
SF House (CT)	7.74	26	33	47	0.2
ANA House (CT)	7.5	232	Not tested	619	0.35
MSA House (four-barrel)	7.78	169	335	577	0.2
MA House (four-barrel)	7.63	18	28	42	0.2
OE House (CT)	6.77	24	95	120	0.2
Date of sampling: 4 September 2007					
SF House (CT)	7.57	20	160	197	0.2
ANA House (CT)	7.66	128	144	699	Not tested
MSA House (four-barrel)	7.36	217	281	728	0.3
MA House (four-barrel)	7.48	46	37	187	0.2
OE House (CT)	7.81	14	23	45	0.2
Average of six rounds of monitoring treated greywater quality	7.47	89	164	523	0.71
Range of values (minimum–maximum)	6.77–7.96	12–312	10–914	36–2,763	0.2–7.79

Table 3.3 Variations of raw and treated greywater

Main parameters of concern	pHunit	TSSmg/l	BODmg/l	CODmg/l
Allowable limit	6–9	150	300	500
Range of values before treatment	5.9–7.8	23–358	110–1,240	92–3,330
Range of values after treatment (minimum–maximum)	6.8–8.00	12–312	10–914	36–2,763

Table 3.4 Results of analysis of heavy metals in a household greywater effluent

Date of effluent sampling: 5 March 2007

Source of sample: OE House

Parameters analysed	Results mg/l	Allowable limits mg/l
Aluminum	0.9	5.0
Arsenic	< 0.005	0.1
Beryllium	< 0.02	0.2
Cadmium	< 0.008	0.01
Chromium	0.16	0.10
Copper	0.1	0.2
Iron	< 0.10	5.0
Lead	1.19	5.0
Lithium	< 0.01	2.5–0.075
Manganese	0.1	0.2
Nickel	2	0.2
Selenium	< 0.005	0.05
Vanadium	0.09	0.1
Zinc	3.23	5.0

Table 3.5 Properties of soil not subject to greywater irrigation

Location	Soil depth cm	Soil extract pH	EC dS/m	SAR	Organic matter %	CaCO3	Soil texture class
Ariha	0–30	7.8	0.42	1.20	2.06	27.27	Silty clayey
Ariha	30–60	7.9	0.62	2.01	1.38		
Al-Jada'a	0–30	7.7	0.36	0.44	3.16	29.95	Clayey
Al-Jada'a	30–60	7.9	0.34	0.49	1.93		

Table 3.6 Olive yield increase due to irrigation with greywater, 2007

Village	Olive age year	Average* yield from olives irrigated with greywater kg/tree	Average* yield from olives not irrigated with greywater kg/tree	Yield increase %
Masa'ar	30	49.5	38.5	28.57
Mugayer	17	56	34.8	60.92
Ariha	10	17.66	13.88	27.23
				Average yield increase 38.9

* Average of yield from 6 olive trees in the same garden

content of these soils ranged from 1.38 to 3.16, which might be attributed to the application of manure as soil enhancer or fertilizers by local people.

Table 3.6 shows that the average olive yield due to complementary irrigation with GW was higher than that of olive trees that did not receive additional water. On average, about a 38.9 per cent increase in olive fruit yield was achieved as a result of complementary irrigation with GW.

The use of compost and soil organic mulching increased plant growth and productivity. Families who owned a GWT unit benefited from the extra water and learned new home garden production methods. Greywater use proved to be a good way for local low-income people to overcome water shortages, increase home garden productivity, and increase the family income.

Table 3.7 shows salinity measured as EC, SAR, and organic matter content of reference soils not irrigated with treated GW, and soils irrigated with treated GW during 2006 and 2007. It was noted that the salinity of soil irrigated with GW increased. It was also noted that EC values increased in three out of five sites in 2007 compared to values in 2006. The increase in EC values in 2007 was less than the increase in EC values in 2006, which could mean that soil salinity stabilized. Irrigation was by low-discharge drippers (8 litres per hour). These types of drippers were found to be suitable because the quantity of irrigation water was limited. But, these drippers were known to result in increased salinity buildup especially in the top soil layer. More monitoring in the future is needed to confirm this conclusion.

Olive trees are moderately salt-tolerant crops. This means that soil salinity values as EC over 5 dS/m could result in reduction of olive tree yield. It also was noted that organic matter content increased in 2006 but decreased in 2007, which could be attributed to the result of the decomposition of

Table 3.7 Results of monitoring greywater impacts on soil EC, SAR, and soil organic matter content

House-hold	Soil depth cm	Reference soils not subject to greywater			Soils after application of greywater in 2006			Soils after application of greywater in 2007		
		EC dS/m	SAR	OM %	EC dS/m	SAR	OM %	EC dS/m	SAR	OM %
1	0–30	0.64	1.85	1.51	1.3	2.01	4.49	2.85	5.71	0.64
	30–60	0.96	2.6	1.38	1.26	1.52	3.49	5.48	7.44	0.56
2	0–30	0.42	1.2	2.06	2.2	0.96	3.07	1.03	1.69	1.06
	30–60	0.62	2.01	1.38	1.69	2.21	3.17	1.21	2.53	1.19
3	0–30	0.51	2	2.89	1.22	2.01	4.26	1.07	1.78	0.89
	30–60	0.57	2.44	1.24	1.61	2.96	5.45	1.37	2.647	0.86
4	0–30	0.7	1.6	4.54	1.22	1.03	3.59	1.56	2.8	0.65
	30–60	0.67	1.85	1.51	1.1	1.61	2.8	1.07	2.84	1.01
5	0–30	0.36	0.44	3.16	1.82	1.45	4.53	2.65	3.21	0.82
	30–60	0.34	0.49	1.93	1.32	2.44	4.53	2.23	4.54	0.79

organic matter. No adverse effects were noted in plant growth during the project period, between 2006 and 2007. Leaching the soil with freshwater is highly recommended to prevent buildup of soil salinity to a degree that could result in reducing crop yield.

The impact of GW irrigation on selected crops was monitored on yearly basis by analysing elements such as nitrogen (N), phosphorous (P), potassium (K), sodium (Na) and chloride (Cl) in olive trees' leaves and fruits. Table 3.8 shows the results of the analysis of leaves and fruits of trees irrigated with treated GW during 2007. No detectable difference was noticed between the nutrient content of olive leaves and fruits of trees irrigated with treated GW and those of trees not irrigated with treated GW. The nutrient content – in the form of N, P, and K – for okra, corn, sunflower and bean irrigated with treated GW was similar to those irrigated with freshwater.

Table 3.9 shows results from the microbiological analysis of okra, corn, sunflower fruits and soil samples during 2007. Both okra and bean fruits must be cooked before consumption. These results indicated that faecal coliform counts were within allowable limits for safe human consumption. As a precaution, all families were trained on the safe harvesting and handling of fruits irrigated with GW. The use of plastic mulching would also reduce the risk of microbiological contamination of garden crops.

Table 3.8 Results of chemical analysis of plants irrigated with treated greywater during 2007

Plant	N%	P%	K%	Na%	Cl%
Okra fruits	2.62	0.362	2.55	0.07	0.84
Okra leaves	2.67	0.231	2.23	0.051	0.86
Bean fruits	2.52	0.43	2.97	0.036	0.97
Bean leaves	3.06	0.50	2.63	0.057	1.97
Corn fruits	2.03	0.314	1.0	0.033	0.21
Corn leaves	1.93	0.371	1.91	0.06	0.83
Sunflower fruits	2.01	0.23	1.92	0.129	0.2
Sunflower leaves	3.17	0.38	3.03	0.055	1.11

Table 3.9 Results of microbiological analysis of plants and soils irrigated with treated greywater during 2007

Type	Total coliform/g	Faecal coliform/g
Okra fruits	1.100	< 3
Okra leaves	< 3	< 3
Bean fruits	4×102	< 3
Bean leaves	4×102	< 3
Corn fruits	4×102	< 3
Corn leaves	> 1,100	> 1,100
Sunflower fruits	93×102	< 3
Sunflower leaves	< 3	< 3
Soil 1	> 16×102	3.5×102
Soil 2	> 16×102	3.5×102

Permaculture practices

Permaculture practices were new to the Karak project community. Such practices are useful to counteract possible salinity impacts of GW use on soil and plants, improve soil productive properties and manage waste generated from GWT and household animals. Soil mulching, a permaculture practice, was made from plant residues, weeds and dry straw. Plant residues 5–10 cm thick were placed under trees on the top soil surface. This helped reduce evaporation of water and decayed into an organic fertilizer.

Rainwater harvesting was attempted to help leach out salts that accumulate from irrigation. Rain was harvested by the construction of a crescent shaped basin – 1.5–2 m in diameter and 15–20 cm in height – around some olive trees. Basins were open from the highest elevation (as a semicircle or a crescent) to direct collected rain to each tree.

Organic mulching with plant residues was introduced once the rain harvesting basin was established around a tree. Table 3.10 shows the effects of mulching on the content of nutrients and calcium carbonate at different soil depths. Mulching increased organic matter and nutrient content of soil by about 43.3 per cent compared to sites with no organic mulching. Organic mulching results in increased soil micro-organism growth and better organic matter decomposition (Foshee et al., 1999).

Soil mulching, accompanied with rainwater harvesting, was implemented to reduce soil salinity and SAR values resulting from GW use. Table 3.11 shows that soil salinity increased by about 1.5 dS/m units as a result of GW application over 3 years.

Table 3.10 Effects of mulching on soil content of nutrients and CaCO3 (2007)

Soil treatment	Soil depth cm	OM %	P ppm	K ppm	N %	$CaCO_3$ %
Mulched soil-1	0–30	0.86	89.4	396.7	0.106	26.4
	30–60	0.86	17.6	231.4	0.090	27.1
Mulched soil-2	0–30	0.86	49.8	184.1	0.106	24.5
	30–60	0.60	14.6	42.3	0.084	22.6
No mulching,	0–30	0.60	4.6	172.3	0.126	23.7
no greywater	30–60	0.26	1.2	65.54	0.084	24.5

Table 3.11 Effects of soil mulching and rain harvesting on soil salinity (2007)

Soil treatment	Soil depth cm	EC dS/m	SAR
Rain harvesting + mulching + greywater, location 1	0–30	1.04	2.14
	30–60	1.00	2.29
Rain harvesting + mulching+ greywater, location 2	0–30	0.85	1.52
	30–60	0.72	1.35
Reference location with no rain harvesting and no greywater	0–30	0.74	1.39
	30–60	0.45	1.79

Field observations also showed that soil organic mulching conserved more soil moisture, when compared with sites of no mulching. Vetch, a legume crop, was planted near trees during the winter season to help nitrogen fixation. The legumes were then incorporated into the top soil layer after flowering. Soil cultivation by legume crops (e.g. vetch) was found essential to increase nitrogen fixation in soil.

Enhancement of the system

One objective of the study was to enhance the design and construction of the four-barrel and CT units so as to obtain GW effluent of a quality suitable for restricted irrigation, to make regular cleaning and maintenance easy to handle by the beneficiaries, and to develop simple techniques and practices to reduce odour and long-term environmental impacts.

The four-barrel type units were in operation for more than six years and the CT units were in operation for about four years. The units performed quite well with regard to the treatment of GW and produced effluents fit for restricted irrigation of crops. However, design improvements and modifications of the GW units was a continuous process. It took more than two years of intensive training after the second year of the Karak project to get the local community to see the benefits of practicing GW treatment and use.

Enhancement of the design and performance of the four-barrel and CT units was necessary to make these units efficient, reliable and of standardized dimensions. It was also important to reduce the cost of construction and operation as much as possible without compromising the performance. Successful efforts were made to improve the performance and efficiency of the GW treatment units and drip irrigation networks, including pipes, impermeable PE sheets, PE barrels, filters for drippers and suitable electric pumps.

Odour control was possible to some extent by improving the GW quality and burying drip irrigation pipes. The beneficiaries were trained on how to control odour by using simple practices and taking continuous care of the units. The beneficiaries were trained to deal with the various reasons for odour emitted from GW, especially at the entrance to the pump that delivers water to the drip irrigation system.

INWRDAM researchers interacted with, and listened to feedback from, technicians and beneficiaries who often pointed out the problems they had faced with the operation and maintenance of these units. Housewives were involved more than male beneficiaries in the day-to-day activities of the project and attended training and community meetings regularly. Housewives considered cleaning and caring for the GW units they owned as a part of their household chores, which generated a new source of irrigation water.

The Karak project's researchers exerted significant effort to develop and improve GWT methods to suit the local rural conditions. The main concerns of the research team included the unavailability and unaffordability of construction materials, and ensuring that unit construction could be carried out by local plumbers, that GW units were easy to operate and maintain, that the unit fitted into a small corner of the home garden, and that GW was treated to quality standards accepted by the users. These constraints were not easy to meet because optimizing a certain set of parameters could negatively influence other parameters. However, improvement of both the four-barrel and the CT GW units was possible since the quality of treated GW produced from these two units was fit for restricted irrigation.

The four-barrel and the CT units share common components such as pipes, a pre-treatment stage, gravel media, pumps, and a drip-irrigation network. At the beginning of the Karak project, the PVC pipes used in the construction of the GWT units were 50 mm in diameter and pipe fittings had 90° bends. Later, problems developed when some pipes were clogged with grease and dirt. The reduction of the frequency of GW pipe clogging was achieved by increasing the size of pipework and fittings from 50 to 75 mm. After test trials in a number of houses for about one year, it was decided to use larger-diameter pipes and smooth bends as an additional precaution to reduce pipe blockages. New rubber seals were fabricated to fit the lager pipe diameter. This modification resulted in a small increase in the cost of units, but helped overcome problems caused by blockages of GW lines.

Incoming GW in earlier types of four-barrel and CT units passed through a first barrel that had a capacity of 160 litres and a depth of 90 cm. Many beneficiaries of the Karak project reported difficulties cleaning this deep barrel where sediments in the bottom could not be easily removed. The cleaning of the first barrel was facilitated by the use of a 50-litre barrel of the same diameter but of a depth of only 50 cm. The retention time of GW in the first barrel was not affected by the reduction of the barrel's capacity because the flow of GW was usually intermittent.

A modification in the CT construction was made to prevent buckling of the pump container, which received treated water from the CT gravel media and helped reduce the possibility of insects getting in and out of the pump container. Before this modification, the pump container was perforated at a certain height to allow treated GW to drain into it from the CT gravel media. These perforations were made using a hand-held electric grinding wheel to make straight cuts around the diameter of the pump container, which weakened the barrel. The result was that some perforations extended to the top of the gravel and allowed insects to pass into the pump tank and sometimes the gravel media pressure resulted in the buckling of the barrel. The modification was made by inserting a 2 m long PVC pipe of a diameter of 75 mm at a fixed height of the barrel and in a level position in the gravel media that allowed treated water to drain from the gravel media to the barrel holding the pump. This modification meant that draining water from the CT gravel media to the barrel holding the pump was always fixed at a pre-determined depth. A small hole of 75 mm diameter did not weaken the barrel.

The gravel media used for the four-barrel and the CT units was inspected regularly for signs of clogging. Some four-barrel and CT units from the Tafila project were monitored to check for media clogging because these units were in operation for a longer time than similar units in the Karak project. Inspection of the gravel medium in a four-barrel unit was conducted by observing signs of clogging – i.e. when incoming GW overflowed across the top the medium without flowing through it. The gravel medium in a CT unit was inspected by removing all the gravel and looking for signs of clogging and compaction. Clogging was more frequent in the four-barrel units than in the CT units. The solution for the prevention of clogging of gravel media was to improve upstream care by the households so as to remove grease and oil from kitchenware before washing with water and to place small screens on sink drains to capture solids and food particles. This will be discussed further below. Washing the gravel media reduced the fines content.

In earlier installations of four-barrel units, the pump was placed at a higher level than the barrels. This resulted in the difficulties with priming the pump when its foot valve stuck or came loose due to corrosion. This problem was overcome by placing the pump level with the base of the last barrel that contained treated GW. This was possible by inserting a 1 inch suction pipe at the bottom of the fourth barrel, which maintained the pump in a flooded and primed condition so that a foot valve was not needed. The only limitation of this arrangement was that the four-barrel unit should be placed over the ground, but this was not always possible. Another solution to the pump priming was to use a submersible pump or a jet pump, but this was an expensive solution.

As a result of improvements in the design of the four-barrel and CT units during the Karak project, it is possible to say that the cost and construction methods of these two types of units were optimized as much as possible without compromising the quality of treated GW.

Financial and economic analysis

The total cost of a GW unit consists of both the capital cost of the unit, including the irrigation network, and the annual operation and maintenance (O&M) costs, such as the cost of electricity for operating the pump. Capital cost estimates for the units were calculated in real term prices for 2006 in Jordan. The total capital cost of the CT and four-barrel units was about US$300 and US$260, respectively. The average annual O&M costs, which were calculated from the O&M costs of units at 60 houses, were about US$39. Table 3.12 shows the breakdown of the actual capital investments for the CT and the four-barrel units based on 2006 prices.

Three types of benefits were identified for such a project – financial, socioeconomic and environmental. The benefit stream appears in the first year following construction and continues till the end of the useable life of the GW units, which is estimated at 10 years.

Financial benefits consist of benefits that have direct market values. These include: 1) additional water (substituting for a component of the existing

Table 3.12 Capital costs of greywater treatment units (based on 2006 Jordan prices)

Item	CT unit US$	4-Four-barrel unit US$	Comments
Labour costs			
Greywater separation inside the household	21.19	21.19	Same for both systems
Site preparation	21.19	14.13	CT needs more excavation
Greywater system installation	42.38	28.25	Technician cost including electrical wiring and drip irrigation
Cost of materials			
3 inch PVC pipes and joints	21.19	21.19	
Rubber seals	4.24	7.10	Four-barrel units use more rubber rings than CT unit
Plastic barrels	16.95	31.10	
PE sheet (4 x 6 m)	28.25	0.00	Needed only for CT units
Submersible pump and wiring	84.75	84.75	
Gravel media	21.19	11.30	
Drip irrigation system for 2,000 m2/50 olive trees	28.25	28.25	Same for both systems
Other costs	14.13	14.13	
Total cost per unit	303.71	261.39	

potable water supply) that could be used by beneficiary groups (water bills for households were used to determine the savings in water consumption); 2) increase in output of the products that were irrigated by GW, e.g. olives; 3) savings due to reducing the frequency of emptying the septic tanks. The average annual total direct revenue for all the surveyed families was estimated at about US$188 per household.

The total direct project costs (cash outflows) included the capital cost of the system at the beginning of the project and annual O&M costs of the unit as well as direct and indirect labour and overhead costs, which were estimated and included in the project cash outflows.

Two main financial indicators were calculated. The net benefits were estimated by subtracting the cash inflows from the cash outflows, and the benefit–cost ratio (B/C) was derived by dividing the cash inflow by the cash outflow. Both indicators were used in the financial analysis.

The following assumptions were adopted for the financial analysis.

- The net present value (NPV) concept was adopted. All inflows and outflows were discounted to the present using the standard methodology.
- The interest rate was assumed to be 3 and 5 per cent, which reflected the opportunity cost of commercial loans in Jordan during 2005–2006 and the public preferences in capital usage.
- The project life-span was assumed either to be 5 or 10 years, where the first year was the zero year (investment year) without being discounted. All the cash inflows and outflows starting the end of the first year were discounted to the base year.

- The following four scenarios were considered: life span of 5 years with interest rate of 5 per cent, life span of 5 years with interest rate of 3 per cent, life span of 10 years with interest rate of 5 per cent, and life span of 10 years with interest rate of 3 per cent.
- The expected benefits and operational costs (cash inflows and outflows) would begin at the end of first year.
- There was no residual book value of infrastructure, machinery and building at the end of project life-cycle.
- Price escalations – the effect of inflation – were not taken into consideration. It was assumed that the differential effect of inflation on operational costs and benefits would be negligible.

The net present value of the costs and benefits was calculated in fixed prices using interest rates of 3 and 5 per cent, with life spans of 5 and 10 years. NPV of the net benefits was the result of subtracting the net present costs from the net present revenues (cash outflows from the cash inflows). The cost calculations in Table 3.13 show average NPV of the costs for the 60 surveyed houses. Table 3.14 shows the total average revenues per family.

Based on the NPV of the revenues and costs, the net present benefits (revenues – costs) and the benefit–cost ratios (B/C) were calculated to reflect the financial feasibility of the project.

Reviewing the details of each sample shows that some (17 out of 60 samples) of the net benefits were negative. However these figures were not considered realistic due to the high costs that were reported by the households, which were between 300 and 400 per cent of the average costs of the majority. However, these abnormal values were not excluded, so as to represent the figures that were reported. The highest net benefits, around US$972, were achieved for the case of 10 year lifetime and 3 per cent interest rate. When applying a 5 per cent interest rate, the net benefits drop by 12.5 per cent. Table 3.15 shows the average net present benefits for the four scenarios considered for this analysis.

Table 3.13 Average net present costs for the 60 surveyed houses

Family number	Net benefits (5 years, 5%) US$	Net benefits (5 years, 3%) US$	Net benefits (10 years, 5%) US$	Net benefits (10 years, 3%) US$
Averages	469	479	600	631

Table 3.14 Average net present benefits (present revenues – present costs) per family

Per family	Net benefits (5 years, 5%) US$	Net benefits (5 years, 3%) US$	Net benefits (10 years, 5%) US$	Net benefits (10 years, 3%) US$
Averages	814	862	1,452	1,605

Table 3.15 Average net present benefits (present revenues – present costs) for four different scenarios

Family number	Net benefits (5 years, 5%) US$	Net benefits (5 years, 3%) US$	Net benefits (10 years, 5%) US$	Net benefits (10 years, 3%) US$
Averages	244.58	270.99	602.71	688.06

Table 3.16 Average values of the benefit–cost ratios for different scenarios

Family number	Net benefits (5 years, 5%) US$	Net benefits (5 years, 3%) US$	Net benefits (10 years, 5%) US$	Net benefits (10 years, 3%) US$
Averages	1.76	1.83	2.58	2.75

The B/C ratios were calculated. A benefit–cost ratio higher than one means that this project will generate net profits at the end of its lifespan. The higher the B/C ratios, the more feasible the project is. Table 3.16 shows average values of the B/C ratios for the different scenarios.

There are other economic benefits that may have resulted from the project, but do not have a direct market value. The use of GW for garden irrigation has the following benefits:

- It saves freshwater that would be otherwise used for irrigation. This is a benefit to the householder, although it is substitutionary since GW can be used only once.
- It reduces the quantities of blackwater that need to be discharged and treated at the central wastewater treatment plant. This is a benefit to the operators of the treatment plant, although there are some concerns that the use of too much GW at the household level will increase the concentration of influent to the treatment plant and require modification of the wastewater treatment process.
- It reduces capital investment in cesspools and costs of emptying them. It is expected that new houses using GW will not need to construct large cesspools and current houses using GW will no longer need to empty their cesspools as frequently as they used to do before the installation of GW units.
- It changes property value. It is likely that the increase in irrigation due to the availability of GW will result in more green areas around the house, which will raise the value of the property.

Unquantified environmental benefits from the project include reducing the risk of contaminating groundwater, which may result from cesspit seepage. However, it was difficult to quantify the impact of the project on groundwater resources as a result of utilizing 80–85 per cent of the generated wastewater, thus preventing its infiltration to groundwater resources. Another positive environmental impact was the enhancement of the local environment around the houses and in the project area in general.

Community participation

The community component of the Karak project addressed elements that would build ownership by the local community and lead to the scale-up of GW use practices by peri-urban communities at the national and regional levels. The community component of the project included training and capacity building of the beneficiaries and local officials to enable them to continue to address their water needs beyond the scope and duration of the project. Meetings were held with local leaders, municipal officials, a local NGO based in Al-Amer villages, a local community-based organization and relevant local government officials in order to raise their awareness and create support to and acceptance of the project among the community.

At the beginning of the Karak project, the LSC was active and showed interest. But, the original composition of the LSC did not include local government agencies who were important stakeholders in the project. The LSC recommended to INWRDAM that more local authorities representing the ministries of Health, Environment, and Agriculture, as well as representative of the local governorate would be useful for the long-term sustainability of the project. Since the recommended agencies were responsible for monitoring health, pollution, and other issues in the governorate, involving them in the LSC would lead to increased horizontal and vertical knowledge sharing and awareness about GW use at the community level. The LSC discussed this idea with the governor of Karak and a new LSC known as the Karak Project Follow-up Committee (KPFC) was formed in July 2006 and included some members of the previous LSC, more beneficiaries, representatives of the ministries of Health, Environment, and Agriculture, of Talal Municipality, and of the local governor.

The establishment of the KPFC resulted in a progressive improvement in the pace of project implementation and better involvement of local community in the activities of the project. Apparently, the beneficiaries were more confident about the project as a result of it being monitored by local government agencies, thus they became more involved in training programmes and in taking care of their units.

The original project plan estimated that about 300 beneficiaries from the 6 villages would be targeted to become beneficiaries. But, this did not happen due to many reasons. Basically, the project took more time than anticipated to sort out the best ways to approach the community and what form the local stakeholder body should take to ensure long-term sustainability. It was found that the Al-Amer community, not including Al-Jada'a Village, had the capacity to uptake only about 110, not 300, GW systems. Although 110 households represent only about 30 per cent of the planned 300 GW units, these represent nearly 50 per cent of the population of Abu-Trabah, Masa'ar,

Mugayer, Ariha and Al-Alia, the five villages of the project area who fulfilled the selection criteria.

It also was observed that many family members become involved in seasonal work, especially during spring time, such as herding and grazing animals and planting wheat. This resulted in less time available for them to attend training and other project activities. To overcome this obstacle, the project team intensified the training of women on O&M and gardening activities, because women usually stay at home most of the time. Therefore, the majority of those regularly attending the training sessions were women and girls. The project team conducted regular visits to beneficiaries and discussed with them how to apply what they had learned. It was apparent that women in the project area were hard working and willing to learn more about GW and ways to support the family income. A number of local technicians, including a female technician, were trained in the installation, operation and maintenance of GW units.

Discussion and recommendations

Project sustainability

One of the important goals of the Karak project was to ensure long-term sustainability of GW use by the community. Owners of GW systems had to show real interest in the system and demonstrate the benefits gained. It was necessary that owners would consider these systems as private household possessions and assets, that they would be willing to contribute effort and money to O&M, and that they would maintain these units in the future. To achieve this goal, the local community was trained in taking proper care of the GW units, in managing their gardens in a way that would reduce long-term impacts of GW on soils and plants, and in installing new GW units.

Community training intensified when most of the GW units were installed and gardening activities were identified. At this stage of the project and after having units installed and in operation for some months, beneficiaries were better able to identify their training needs. Training focused on solving real problems faced by the community of GW users, and the trainers were able to develop and improve the training content accordingly. Beneficiaries were informed how to deal with GW treatment and use for irrigation.

A direct positive impact that resulted from having more than 110 households in Al-Amer villages practising GW use was the significant reduction of the need for additional domestic water supply during summer months. The local governor had opened a dedicated office to respond to complaints about water shortages. An employee working at the local governorate offices and in charge of following up on water shortage complaints during summer months informed INWRDAM that the offices did not receive many complaints from Al-Amer villages in 2006 and 2007. Since no change occurred in the water supply situation, he attributed the reason for the decrease in the number of complaints about water shortages to the GW project helping the Al-Amer community offset the demand with the use of GW for irrigation.

In December 2006, INWRDAM carried out a monitoring survey that covered 60 out of the 110 household beneficiaries at Al-Amer villages. The survey results indicated that the agriculture component of the project achieved the expected results and that GW users were satisfied with the noticeable improvement in the growth of trees and garden crops. The majority of respondents indicated that they had learned new methods of cropping and irrigation and that their awareness of GW use increased. A majority of respondents (98 per cent) indicated that they would be able to sustain the GW systems after the conclusion of the project. Ninety-five per cent of the respondents said they consider their GW systems as their personal possessions and 87 per cent said they would encourage their relatives and friends to use GW. Two-thirds of the respondents (72 per cent) said they had access to a trained local technician to conduct O&M if needed.

Some women were identified for more specific training that would improve their skills as 'local leader women'. At the conclusion of the project, a number of local women, most of whom owned GW units, decided to join their efforts and combine financial resources to establish and register the first local women's cooperative in the area. The main aim of this cooperative was to promote GW use and other development activities in their community.

Conclusion

The four years of research activities conducted during the Karak project have resulted in a vast amount of data and information related to the different aspects of GW use for irrigation in the rural areas of Jordan. The Karak project was characterized – when compared with previous similar research projects – by the number of partners and stakeholders involved in the implementation of different activities of the project. This project included different research fields, such as water policy, socioeconomy, health, agriculture and the environment. With water scarcity considered a high priority in Jordan, one can say that the Karak project was a model and clear example for the implementation of Integrated Water Resource Management (IWRM) and water demand management (WDM) principles.

The following conclusions and recommendations can be stated as an outcome of the Karak project.

- At a policy level, stakeholder government institutions became more aware of the importance of the potential of GW treatment and use. Future GW research and implementation should involve the government sector as a contributor and an implementer.
- At a community level, the Al-Amer communities were introduced to intensive training and capacity-building programmes on issues related to

GW use, creating an enabling environment favourable to future development opportunities in the project area.

- At a technical level, building upon previous GW research outcomes conducted by INWRDAM, the use of low-cost GW treatment units proved to be feasible and realistic in rural houses.
- Permaculture practices and new crops were introduced to the Karak project communities.

Specific conclusions

- Greywater treatment units were well accepted by the majority of households of Al-Amer villages. Future efforts should focus on widening the number of rural communities practising GW use.
- Based on the limited data available, GW treatment and use proved to be economically feasible with an average B/C ratio of 2.75, based on estimation of the average of 56 out of 110 beneficiaries. It is recommended that all GW research includes economic feasibility as a basic part of the research proposal.
- The adoption of GW use guidelines for rural areas in Jordan by JISM under code JS1776:2008 was a direct outcome of the activities of the Karak project. Future proposals should include objectives to concentrate efforts to adopt other related codes and guidelines, such as environment-friendly detergents and building codes.
- The average quantity of treated GW was 237 litres/day/household. This was available round the year and is sufficient to irrigate about 20 olive trees.

The Water Authority of Jordan (WAJ) was interested in the activities of the Karak project and monitored the quality of the GW discharged from a number of houses in the project. Based on records of the treated GW quality obtained from 63 houses, WAJ prepared and submitted a proposal to the Jordanian Institute for Standardization and Metrology recommending that the Institute issue GW use guidelines in rural areas of Jordan. These guidelines were adopted as JS 1776:2008 in late 2008.

Recommendations

- Greywater research is in its infancy in the MENA region and must be intensified so it becomes fully integrated in the activities of higher learning and specialized government intuitions.
- Impacts of GW use for irrigation on the environment must be monitored and evaluated so that better understanding of constraints are identified and assessed.
- Health impacts of GW use on farmers and consumers of products irrigated with GW must be identified through sound epidemiological studies.

- Sanitary building codes that enforce and/or subsidize separation of GW are needed in the MENA region to encourage more households and institutions to separate and use GW.
- Intensive research activities are needed, leading to the design of GW and wastewater treatment methods suitable for irrigation and indoor use so as to save freshwater.
- Greywater use should be seen both as a strategy to address water scarcity and a poverty-alleviation strategy. Any technology intervention should be cost effective while meeting accepted standards (see Aqaba Declaration in this volume).

Acknowledgements

The reported research findings are the outcome of a project entitled Greywater Treatment and Reuse for Poverty Reduction in Jordan (Phase II), which was conducted by the Inter-Islamic Network on Water Resources Development and Management (INWRDAM), Amman, Jordan, during 2004–2007, with a grant from the International Development Research Centre (IDRC), Ottawa, Canada. Thanks are due to our partners in the project, NCARRT, LSC, and the people of the local communities in the project areas.

References

Center for the Study of the Built Environment (CSBE) (2003) *Greywater Reuse in Other Countries and Its Applicability to Jordan* [online], available from: http://www.csbe.org/graywater/contents/htm [accessed 6 January 2009].

Foshee, W.G., Goff. W.D., Patterson, M.G., Tilt, K.M., Dozier, W.A. Jr., Truker, L.S. and Bannon, J.S. (1999) 'Organic mulches affect soil and leaf nutrient levels of young pecan trees', *Journal of Arboriculture* 25: 81–4.

Gross, A., Azulai, N., Oron, G., Ronen, Z., Arnold, M. and Nejidat, A. (2005) 'Environmental impacts and health risks associated with greywater irrigation: A case study', *Water Science and Technology* 52:161–9.

Halalsheh, M., Dalahmeh S., Sayed M., Suleiman W., Shareef M., Mansour M. and Safi M. (2008) 'Greywater characteristics and treatment options for rural areas in Jordan', *Bioresources Technology* 99: 6635–41.

Inter-Islamic Network on Water Resources Development and Management (INWRDAM) (2003) *Permaculture and Greywater and Reuse Project, Tafila, Jordan.* [Unpublished project final report]

INWRDAM (2007) *Greywater Treatment and Use for Poverty Reduction in Jordan (Phase II).* [Unpublished project final report]

Jamrah, A., Al-Omari, A., Al-Qasem, L. and Abdel Ghani, N. (2006) 'Assessment of availability and characteristics of grey water in Amman', *Water International* 31: 210–20.

Jordanian Institute for Standards and Metrology (JSIM) (2006) *Jordan Standard, No 893.2006.*

Metcalf and Eddy (2003) *Wastewater Engineering: Treatment, Disposal, Reuse,* 4th edn, McGraw-Hill, New York.

PLAN:NET (2004) *Post Project Evaluation of Greywater Treatment and Reuse Project in Tafila, Jordan*. [Unpublished project final report]

Redwood, M. (2007) 'Greywater use in the Middle East and North Africa region', *Greywater Stock-taking Meeting, IDRC–CSBE*, Aqaba, Jordan.

Water Authority of Jordan (WAJ) (2005) *Annual Report*, Amman.

World Health Organisation (WHO) (2006) *Guidelines for the Safe Use of Wastewater, Excreta and Greywater* (vols 1–4), WHO, Geneva.

About the authors

Dr Bino is the Executive Director of INWRDAM. He has held positions as a senior researcher at the Royal Scientific Society in Amman; a director of Industrial Chemistry; and a director of the Environmental Research Centre. Email: muradinw@nic.net.jo

Shihab Beiruti is a research scientist with INWRDAM, and has been working on the GW project since 2001.

Mohammad Ayesh is a permaculture specialist at the National Center for Agricultural Research and Extension (NCARE), formerly known as the National Centre for Agricultural Research and Technology Transfer (NCARTT), and has been cooperating with INWRDAM in the implementation of GW agricultural related activities since 2003.

CHAPTER 4

Greywater management in the northeastern Badia of Jordan

Wael Suleiman, Bassam Al-Hayek, Moayied Assayed, Sahar Dalahmeh and Nisreen Al-Hmoud

This chapter looks at the feasibility of adopting non-conventional GW manage-ment policies for small, rural communities in the north-eastern Badia of Jordan. The north-eastern Badia comprises 33 small clusters (communities), all of which lack public sewerage networks. The most common wastewater collection method is the use of pit latrines and unlined cesspools. About two-thirds of the population separate GW from blackwater, but use the GW for irrigation in an uncontrolled manner and without any treatment. A local stakeholder committee (LSC) formed of and including community members and officials was engaged in all project activities, including field visits to wastewater/GW treatment-and-use projects as well as a training workshop on public participation concepts and participatory rapid (or rural) appraisal (PRA) tools and methodologies. Relevant social, eco-nomic, and environmental data and information were collected utilizing PRA tools as well as formal surveys. One of the clusters – Rawdat Al-Amir Ali – was appointed as a research site based on specific criteria set by the research team and the LSC. Greywater quality and quantities generated from different fixtures of six households at the research site were investigated during the period March–August 2005. Different cost-effective and technologically-sound alternative treatment op-tions were assessed, taking into consideration potential reuse opportunities. Two different treatment options were considered: 1) septic tank followed by intermit-tent sand filter; 2) up-flow anaerobic sludge blanket (UASB). Two pilot plants were designed, installed and operated in two households at the research site.

Introduction

The population of Jordan was estimated at 5.2 million in 2001, with an urban/rural balance of approximately 78 per cent/22 per cent. People in small, rural communities are located in about 1,145 clusters scattered all over the country (Table 4.1). These communities generally lack public sewerage ser-vices. Inhabitants rely mainly on inadequately managed on-site wastewater disposal systems that fail to protect the scarce water resources, public health and safety, and the surrounding environment because of the discretionary

Table 4.1 Population distribution (2001)

Population range	No. of communities	Population
> 50,000	17	1,888,500
10,000–50,000	91	1,740,700
5,000–10,000	81	532,140
< 5,000	1,145*	1,020,660

* Considered small communities
Source: Department of Statistics, 2002

manner in which these systems have been designed, installed and managed (WHO, 2000).

The country is facing a future of very limited water resources, among the lowest in the world on a per-capita basis. Although access to safe drinking-water supplies has been impressive, reaching over 96 per cent of the population, the expansion of modern sanitation systems to meet public health and environmental goals has lagged significantly behind, particularly in rural marginalized areas. This is mainly attributed to the present wastewater management policies that rely on centralized systems, hampering the extension of this service to small rural communities where inhabitants live in dwellings scattered over large areas. Interest in adopting non-conventional wastewater management strategies for small un-sewered communities in Jordan is rapidly increasing. However, this has not yet been investigated in an integrated framework (Al-Jayyousi, 2003).

The research investigated, in close consultation and with the active participation of the community, the feasibility of adopting innovative GW management policies for small rural communities in the country. This was approached through a coherent framework of activities, including the integration of various components of social, technical, economical, environmental and public participation requirements.

Methodology

The study area is the northeastern Badia that covers an area of about 25,600 km², which is 28 per cent of the total area of the country, with a population of 25,820 in 2001 living in 33 clusters (Department of Statistics, 2002). The word Badia means the place where Bedouin people live. In the past, Bedouins were more nomadic than they are today. In recent times, their lifestyle has become more sedentary, requiring more infrastructure, facilities and services.

Community participation

Site visits to most of the communities in the study area were organized. Meetings were held with community leaders and representatives, municipality directors, principals of girls' and boys' schools and representatives of non-governmental organizations (NGOs) and community-based organizations

(CBOs) to introduce the study idea, objectives, methodology of work and the role of the community.

A local stakeholder committee (LSC) was formed by the communities in the area. The committee comprised 15 people, 4 women and 11 men, from different communities in the study area. The LSC was involved in different activities of the project. The researchers and the LSC met regularly and discussed various issues related to the project, including the technical aspects.

To build capacity among the public on different aspects of participatory development communication, the research team, in cooperation with external specialists, held a training workshop for four days at one of the CBO premises in the project area. The training focused on the concept of participation and participatory rapid (or rural) appraisal (PRA) tools and methodologies that could be used to identify wastewater problems and solutions based on the community's perspectives and needs. There was an emphasis on the more salient issues such as inhabitants' perceptions of water scarcity, GW use at the household level as an effective water demand management strategy and onsite wastewater management practices.

Domestic visits to wastewater treatment and use projects

Five field trips were organized for LSC and other community representatives in order to develop community-based 'know-how' and to share knowledge between the community and the research team that could help understand the issues and constraints faced in the setup and operation of wastewater treatment-and-use systems for small communities. The first visit was to the western part of the country, Deir Alla, where the Canadian International Development Agency (CIDA) funded a wastewater treatment-and-use project for an area comprising 13 communities with a total population of about 6,000. The second trip was to the southern part of Jordan, Wadi Mousa, where a treatment-and-use project, funded by the United States Agency for International Development (USAID), has been operating since 2001 and serving three small communities. Two other field visits were organized to a university campus in the northern part of the country and to a nearby treatment-and-use project serving three small communities and a refugee camp. The fifth field visit was to small communities in the southern part of Jordan, Karak and Tafila cities, where the International Development Research Centre (IDRC), Canada, funded a GW treatment-and-use project for several communities in the area.

Data collection

Utilizing information obtained during the PRA training workshop, the researchers and LSC prepared a checklist to identify social, economic, environmental and technical issues related to the study based on the community's perspectives and needs. The checklist, shown in Table 4.2, was used as a tool to guide the team in collecting data during field visits to households.

A work plan was prepared to cover the project area, with an aim to include 8–15 per cent of the population in data collection. Work teams were formulated; each consisted of 3–5 members, including at least one female member and a member of the research team. Each work team was assigned a study area with a minimum number of meetings to be conducted. A total of 404 meetings

Table 4.2 Checklist prepared and used by the local stakeholder committee

	Suggested questions and topics	Source of data	PRA tools to be used
Social issues	Number of family members and their educational levels Number of wives Income sources and rates Frequency and cost of cesspool pump-outs	Parents Family members	Semi-structured dialogue Direct observations
Economic issues	Planted area around the residence and water sources for irrigation Number of owned livestock and drinking water sources	Parents	Semi-structured dialogue Direct observations
General available services	Availability of different services (e.g. charity societies, streets, schools, health-care centres, drinking-water networks, electricity, telephone networks, etc.)	Individuals Groups Municipality Charity association	Semi-structured dialogue Direct observations
Environmental issues	Current wastewater disposal practices and adverse impacts on public health and the environment (potential groundwater pollution) How do you perceive the impacts of using treated wastewater for irrigation? Do you separate wastewater coming out of the kitchen and the bathroom (GW) from that of the toilet? If yes, why and how do you get rid of it? Are there any GW use practices? Are these planned or not? Do you accept reusing treated wastewater for irrigation?Do you prefer to treat and use GW or wastewater as a whole? What is the frequency of cesspool pump-outs? How much does this cost you? What is the distance between your residence and the dumping site? What wastewater management alternatives do you suggest?	Individuals Family members Groups Municipality Charity associations	Semi-structured dialogue Ranking, Problem and solution network Mapping Direct observations Seasonal calendar Historical background Daily routine
Water issues	Is the municipal water supply adequate? Any other alternatives? How much does municipal water cost you? What are the differences in water consumption between summer and winter?	Family members Groups Municipality Charity associations	Semi-structured dialogue Direct observations Seasonal calendar Historical background Daily routine

were carried out during 13 days of field work. In addition, a formal survey was conducted to collect relevant data and information utilizing questionnaires.

Identification of an appropriate community

The authors set criteria to identify one community within the project area as the research site where pilot field-experiments for GW collection, treatment and use were to be conducted. These criteria included:

- the opportunity to improve current wastewater management practices;
- social acceptance and favourability for use;
- representation and potential for replication;
- institutional support and the presence of NGOs and/or CBOs.

Together with the LSC, the researchers reviewed the data and information collected to screen the communities. A considerable number of communities were excluded due to the fact that favourability for use was limited either due to the type of soil or because of the limited agricultural activities. Other sites were excluded because of the limited potential for replication in areas that do not adequately represent the project area (in terms of population and income rate). Some communities were also rejected due to the lack of NGOs and/or CBOs that could provide appropriate institutional support.

The group selected a list of seven communities. Site visits were conducted to these communities and further screening was carried out. Finally, the group decided to identify Rawdat Al-Amir Ali as the research-project site.

Greywater quality and quantity

There are three modes used to collect GW generated from households at the research site. These are: collecting all the generated GW at one discharge point; collecting water coming out of the kitchen in one point, and other GW sources in another point; and collecting water coming out of the kitchen, water coming out of ablution and hand washing and other GW sources in separate discharge points.

Quality and quantities of GW discharged at the different points were investigated during the period March–August 2005. A total of six households, each following the same trend of GW separation, were selected in cooperation with the LSC for this purpose. Generated quantities were measured on a daily basis, while composite samples were collected bimonthly from each discharge point. Samples were carefully placed in containers and kept in an ice-box at a temperature of less than 4°C. All analytical tests were performed in accordance with the Standard Methods for The Examination of Water and Wastewater (APHA et al., 1998).

Selection of the appropriate treatment system

A literature survey was conducted that included studying many of the low-cost technologically-sound treatment alternatives that are/were used on a small scale as on-site or decentralized treatment systems, taking into consideration potentials of reusing reclaimed water. In order to evaluate each of the treatment options mentioned above, certain selection criteria were set taking into consideration GW quality and quantity, community requirements, and local regulations. In addition, an expert group consisting of the research team, local wastewater treatment-and-use experts and a representative of the LSC was formulated to establish a network for discussion, information exchange, assessment, and evaluation of affordable and attractive options for GW treatment that are suitable for the local environment/social conditions.

Results

Social, economic and environmental information

The total population of the study area was estimated at 28,480 in 2004, distributed in 33 small clusters. The society is characterized as a youthful one with more than 40 per cent of the population under the age of 15. About 18.5 per cent of the population is illiterate, and the average number of family members is nine. The average monthly income rate is estimated at JOD123 per family (base on exchange rates of May 2009, JOD1 = US$1.41).

The study area suffers from a water shortage problem. Domestic water is being supplied through the public network for only 24 hours a week and inhabitants purchase water from the private sector particularly in the summer period. People spend around 5 per cent of their income on their water bill. Agricultural activities in the area are limited and only possible through irrigation. Wheat and barley are the main crops grown. The main obstacle facing agriculture in the area is water scarcity.

The community relies mainly on unlined cesspools as an on-site wastewater collection system. Cesspools at some clusters are rarely emptied, and at other clusters are pumped out on a monthly basis, with an average entailed cost of JOD21. The closest legal liquid-waste dumping site is 80 km away from the area and inhabitants believe that wastewater pumped out of cesspools is being illegally disposed of in nearby streams. About 62 per cent of the public in the study area utilize pit latrines or ventilated improved pit latrines, 33 per cent have traditional (no-flush) indoor toilets, and only 1 per cent use a flush toilet (compared to 89 per cent on the national level). Only 40 per cent of the community have showers and kitchen sinks.

As for GW, two-thirds of the community indigenously separate GW from blackwater, mainly for religious reasons. Greywater is being used directly and without any treatment for irrigating planted areas in the backyards in an uncontrolled manner, paying no formal attention to health aspects.

Greywater quality and generation rates

During the period March–August 2005, GW quantities generated at the six dwellings involved in the study were measured on a daily basis. Some relevant information was also collected, such as number of family members, number of children per family, type of toilet used and the availability of showers and/or bathing tubs. In addition, composite samples over a 24-hour period were collected bimonthly and analysed for physical, chemical and microbial constituents.

Greywater generation rates ranged from 12.0–19.0 litres/capita/day (l/c/d). Quantities generated from the kitchen comprised about 50 per cent of the total GW quantity generated from all the discharge points, while the quantities generated from ablution and hand washing were the lowest. The highest generation rate was for a household that had an indoor toilet. Lower generation rates were observed for households that did not have showers or basins for bathing.

The results from the survey conducted on GW quality are shown in Table 4.3. They indicate that the quality varied highly among the common collection points (same sources of GW) in different households. This was mainly attributed to the different activities that were undertaken during sampling (e.g. washing clothes, washing floors and others). The fat, oil and grease (FOG) content was found to be higher than that in wastewater generated in other communities, particularly urban ones. This could be attributed to the food style and meal patterns. The organic content was higher for GW coming out of the kitchen than other GW sources. The levels were higher for households with higher numbers of children. One of the practices in such communities is that mothers do not use nappies for children, and it is common practice to clean children in basins that led to GW discharge points. It was also quite common for inhabitants to wash their hands in the ablution basins or kitchen sinks after going to pit latrines or toilets. *Escherichia coli* (*E. coli*) levels were also higher than expected even for GW coming out of the kitchen sinks and ablution basins.

Levels of macro-nutrients (nitrogen T-N, phosphorous T-P, and potassium K) were lower for water generated from the kitchen sinks and ablution basins compared to levels for water generated from other sources. The pH levels of GW collected from the kitchen sinks were lower than those of water generated from other sources. This was found to be in agreement with results obtained by other researchers (Burnat, 1997; Dixon et al., 1999a, b).

Comparing the microbial quality of GW with the World Health Organization (WHO) guidelines of 1989 for the use of wastewater in irrigation, it is likely that GW quality at all discharge points is suitable only for restricted irrigation, i.e. of cereal crops, industrial and fodder crops, pasture and trees. According to the WHO guidelines, it is not recommended to use such water to irrigate crops likely to be eaten uncooked, sports fields and public parks. The guidelines also impose site restrictions and recommend people not to

Table 4.3 Greywater quality generated at different discharge points

Parameter	Unit	Site code*											
		A	B	C	D	E	F	G	H	I	J	K	L
pH	SU	5.5	7.3	5.8	7.2	7.0	5.7	5.6	8.3	7.3	5.4	6.9	8.2
EC	µs/cm	870	2,422	875	2,373	2,100	1,560	1,357	2,812	1,286	1,163	859	2,496
TDS	mg/l	649	1,409	821	1,724	1,140	1,007	918	1,271	793	934	567	1,138
TSS	mg/l	655	1,789	527	1,569	700	990	410	698	810	985	448	558
BOD5	mg/l	827	1,285	832	1,423	977	1,134	1,092	650	657	1,648	544	716
COD	mg/l	1,852	3,202	1,930	5,501	2,257	2,878	2,085	1,915	1,543	3,109	1,063	1,745
T Kj N	mg/l	31	186	33	90	161	94	80	177	75	58	33	200
T-P	mg/l	32	25	9	25	16	23	13	34	25	19	18	29
K	mg/l	9	21	10	7	27	21	6	11	20	17	11	31
MBAS	mg/l	46	77	88	207	45	33	36	43	53	51	12	54
E. coli	MPN/100 ml	2.5E+05	1.7E+05	6.6E+04	1.0E+06	3.9E+04	2.8E+05	1.9E+04	4.7E+04	2.3E+04	2.5E+06	7.2E+03	6.4E+05
B	mg/l	0.8	0.8	0.6	0.7	1.0	0.7	1.7	1.6	1.0	0.6	0.4	0.6
FOG	mg/l	124	257	226	405	202	319	147	164	91	85	84	67

* A, C, G, and J: kitchen sink only; B and D: all greywater except the kitchen sink; E and F: total greywater; H and K: ablution and hand washing; I and L: greywater other than the kitchen and ablution sinks.

be exposed to such water unless they wear gloves and have safety shoes. The project team illustrated this to the LSC members during one of the meetings. It is worth mentioning that unrestricted irrigation, according to the aforementioned WHO guidelines, applies only for water with less than 1,000 MPN/100 ml of total thermo-tolerant coliform count TTCC (or *E. coli*) and of $\leq$ 1.0 egg of intestinal pathogenic nematodes/l.

Treatment options and pilot experiments

The following design criteria were adopted for identifying appropriate treatment options:

- BOD_5 = 1,000 mg/l;
- TSS = 750 mg/l;
- GW generation rate = 200 litres/family/day;
- reclaimed water is to be used for restricted irrigation.

The study team, including the local expert group, developed an evaluation matrix to assess different treatment alternatives as shown in Tables 4.4 and 4.5. The team was in favour of utilizing one or more of the following treatment options, taking into account the socioeconomic characteristics of the study area an up-flow anaerobic sludge blanket (UASB) or septic tank followed by intermittent sand filter.

Two pilot plants were designed, constructed, and operated during the period March–August 2006. Design drawings for sand filter and UASB units are shown in Figures 4.1 and 4.2, respectively. The performance of each plant in treating generated GW was evaluated and the results are shown in Table 4.6. The septic tank/sand filter system gave a high performance in removing organic and solid contents. BOD_5 and TSS reductions of 86 per cent and 81 per cent were demonstrated, with effluent concentrations of 67 mg/l and 37 mg/l respectively. In addition, *E. coli* counts were drastically reduced by four logs to levels below 1,000 MPN/100 ml. The UASB system indicated high performance as well with BOD_5 and TSS reductions of 79 per cent and 87 per cent for effluent concentrations of 223 mg/l and 80 mg/l, respectively. However, this system showed a lower *E. coli* reduction compared to the septic tank/sand filter system.

The performance of UASB in removing pathogens improved upon the provision of the unit with a small filter of zeolite. The zeolite filter not only improved the pathogenic removal, but it also markedly improved the removal of organic matter and suspended solids, detergent, oil, and grease (the overall efficiency is shown in Table 4.7).

According to the WHO guidelines for the use of reclaimed water mentioned earlier, effluent coming from the intermittent sand filter is suitable for unrestricted irrigation. However, the community was oriented to use reclaimed GW for restricted irrigation only. This is mainly due to the fact that Jordanian regulations do not allow the use of reclaimed water for unrestricted irrigation

Table 4.4 Selection matrix of the greywater treatment system

Type of system	Source characteristics			Community requirements					
	Effectiveness in handling high organic loads yes/no	Effectiveness in removing BOD, TSS, FOG, N, and pathogens %	Ability to operate under variable flow patterns, shock loads yes/no	Land requirement m²	Production of odours yes/no	Maintenance requirement daily, weekly, monthly, or yearly	Operation requirements Is it a user-friendly system? yes/no	Approximate construction cost JOD	Approximate operation cost JOD
Septic tank	Yes	BOD: 35% TSS: 40%	Yes	3 m³	Yes, ventilation is required	Yearly de-sludging	No operation requirements	400 (plastic tank, fittings, excavation)	20 per year (for de-sludging)
Intermittent sand filter (preceded by septic tank)	No	BOD: 90% TSS: 80%	Yes	10 m²	Yes if open filter	Monthly	Yes, but needs operational requirements for laterals, sprinklers, backwashing	400	
Wetland	No	BOD: 40% TSS: 44% N: 33% pathogens: 71%	Yes, need stabilization tank	25 m² / 2 m³ 1–2 m² / 200 1	No	Monthly harvesting	No operation requirement, but is still not user friendly	120 per m²	20 per month (harvesting) +200 (zeolite replacement)
Sequencing batch reactor	Yes	BOD: 85% TSS: 85% No nitrogen removal	No, need stabilization tank	2 m²	No	Monthly	Yes, power supply, daily de-sludging	> 1,000 (air blowers, diffusers, and pneumatic valves)	Power, sludge disposal
Up-flow anaerobic sludge blanket	Yes	COD: 75–90%	Yes	Reactor of (350-litre capacity, with height of 2 m)	No	De-sludging every 2 years (100 litres/ year)	No operation requirement, user friendly	300	Zero

Table 4.5 Selection matrix of the greywater treatment system (cont'd)

Type of system	Use opportunity and local regulations	Receiving environment		Availability of construction materials/treatment media in the study area (Yes/No)
	Effluent quality meets the Jordanian Specification (893/2002) for Restricted Irrigation yes/no	Losses (evaporation, evapo-transpiration) high, moderate, low	Need for specific environmental conditions (temperature, topography) yes/no	
Septic tank	No	Low	Temp > 15°C	Yes
Intermittent sand filter (preceded by septic tank)	Yes	Moderate	No	Yes
Wetland	Yes, but depends on surface area of wetland	High	No	Yes
Sequencing batch reactor	Yes except for nitrogen and COD	Low	Topography: SBR has to be mounted above ground surface to facilitate de-sludging	No
Up-flow anaerobic sludge blanket	Yes	Low	Optimum temperature is 35°C; isolation is recommended	Yes

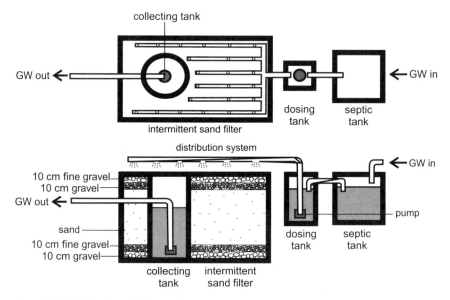

Figure 4.1 Septic tank-sand filter unit

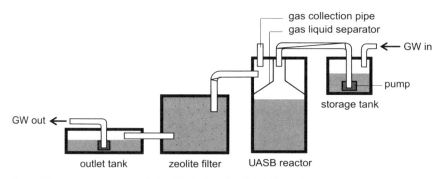

Figure 4.2 Up-flow anaerobic sludge blanket sludge (UASB) reactor

regardless of its quality, and also to minimize potential health risks that could arise due to improper operational manners.

A training seminar on the construction, operation, and maintenance of GWT units was organized. The seminar targeted community members (men and women) and aimed at building up the knowledge and hands-on expertise of the sand filters and UASB treatment units.

Table 4.6 Performance of septic tank/sand filter system

Parameter	Unit	JS(893/2006) Use for fodder and industrial crops and cooked vegetables (maximum allowable limit)	Septic tank/intermittent sand filter			
			Raw greywater	Effluent from septictank	Effluent from sandfilter	Overall efficiency %
BOD5	mg/l	300	1,182	438	59	95
COD	mg/l	500	2,248	951	161	93
TSS	mg/l	300	609	206	31	95
FOG	mg/l	8	159	17	8	95
MBAS	mg/l	100	27	39	12	53
NO3-N	mg/l	10	47	2	1	98
NH3-N	mg/l	–	53	100	50	5
T Kj N	mg/l	–	112	108	50	56
T-N	mg/l	70	211	210	101	52
T-P	mg/l	30	20	19	8	57
SAR	Unitless	9	7	6	4	40
E. coli	MPN/100 ml	–	2.17E+03	5.86E+05	2.27E+02	90

– no limits in the standard

Table 4.7 Performance of UASB/zeolite system

Para-meter	Unit	JS (893/2006) Use for fodder and industrial crops and cooked vegetables (maximum allowable limits)	UASB/zeolite filter					
			Effluent from storage tank	Effluent from UASB	Effluent from zeolite filter	Efficiency of UASB %	Efficiency of zeolite filter %	Overall efficiency %
BOD5	mg/l	300	1,051	291	223	72	23	79
COD	mg/l	500	2,030	761	429	63	44	79
TSS	mg/l	300	596	137	80	77	42	87
FOG	mg/l	8	136	76	8	44	89	94
MBAS	mg/l	100	37	14	11	63	18	70
NO3-N	mg/l	10	3	0	1	99	**	63
NH3-N	mg/l	–	5	5	4	2	19	20
T Kj N	mg/l	–	36	13	15	63	**	58
T-N	mg/l	70	44	18	20	58	**	54
T-P	mg/l	30	12	4	2	65	42	80
SAR	Unitless	9	5	9	2	**	82	65
E. coli	MPN/100 ml	–	1.74E+06	5.17E+06	2.22E+05	**	96	87

** no removal of pollutant occurred
– no limits in the standard

Cost–benefit analysis of the two selected treatment units

The use of treated GW benefited the targeted households in reducing the domestic water consumption rates, thus saving the household some money for other purposes. On the other hand, the availability of such an alternative resource increased the farming productivity particularly in terms of olives and olive oil. A simple cost–benefit analysis of the two scenarios of treatment is shown in Tables 4.8 and 4.9.

From economic and water-saving points of view and based on the cost–benefit analysis, it was found that a treatment unit that serves a group of houses is more feasible than one that serves a single house, as the costs will be shared among the group and the generated water quantities will be higher. Moreover, the savings on water bills will be more substantial for a group of houses than for a single house.

Conclusion

Participatory approaches, taking into account the knowledge and experience of local people, need to be applied when investigating integrated water-resources management programmes for small communities. In this respect, intensive awareness campaigns are essential to inform the communities of current issues and new trends in water-resource management. Field visits of local people to wastewater treatment-and-use projects are important to develop community-

Table 4.8 Cost–benefit analysis of UASB treatment unit

Scenarios	Costs and benefits	UASB unit cluster of 4 houses
Saving on water bill	Cost of unit (JOD)	613
+	Water saving (m3/ year)	144
Production of olive oil	Saving on water Bill (JOD/year)	49.6
	Olive oil production (no. of tank/year)	5
	Cost of olive oil (JOD/year)	250
	Total benefit (JOD/year)	299.6
	Payback period (year)	2.04

Table 4.9 Cost–benefit analysis of septic tank/sand filter treatment unit

Scenarios	Costs and benefits	Sand filter unit
Saving of Water Tankers costs	Cost of unit (JOD)	834
+	Water saving (m3/ year)	54
Production of Olive Oil	Cost of water tankers (JOD/year)	121.5
	Olive oil production (no. of tank/year)	1
	Cost of olive oil (JOD/year)	50
	Total benefit (JOD/year)	171.5
	Payback period (year)	4.86

based know-how and to share knowledge and ideas. All of these actions form a new base of knowledge and sound management experience, tailored to the needs and situation of the communities in consideration.

Greywater is a vital and sustainable water resource that should receive considerable attention when targeting wastewater management in small communities. Greywater treatment and use for irrigation could be an effective water-demand management strategy for small clusters in Jordan. However, the practices and habits of the community highly affect both GW generation rates and GW quality, particularly in terms of microbial and organic contents. Current practices of GW use need to be improved, taking into consideration health aspects.

Based on the treatment technology selection matrix, which was developed by the project team and the expert committee with participation of LSC representatives, it was found that two treatment technologies can be used to treat GW generated in small rural communities in the Badia of Jordan. These are: 1) septic tank followed by intermittent sand filter (ISF); 2) septic tank followed by an up-flow anaerobic sludge blanket (UASB). The septic tank followed by intermittent sand filter showed high performance in treating GW in terms of physical, chemical, and microbial aspects. The sand filter was very effective in removing the pathogens indicated by *E. coli*. The performance of the UASB system in removing pathogens was improved after providing the system with a post treatment zeolite filter. Although both systems were efficient in treating fairly contaminated GW, the UASB coupled with a zeolite filter was easier to operate and maintain, and was more cost effective.

Reclaimed water from the systems investigated could be used for restricted irrigation. On a family level, it can be said that GW use can contribute somehow to improving food security (olive fruit and olive oil) and enhance the household income.

Acknowledgements

This research study was conducted by the Environmental Research Center of the Royal Scientific Society, under a grant from the International Development Research Centre (IDRC), Canada. The authors appreciate the support of Dr. Lamia El Fattal, senior program officer at IDRC. Grateful acknowledgement is made to Eng. Othman Mashaqbeh and the environmental and socioeconomic team of the Royal Scientific Society who participated in the research activities.

The team also acknowledges the cooperation of CARE International in Jordan/CARE Australia and PLAN:NET, Canada, for designing and implementing a training workshop for four days at one of the CBOs in the project area.

Grateful appreciation also is extended to all members of the communities and public organizations who participated and contributed to the success of this research study.

References

Al-Jayyousi, O.R. (2003) 'Greywater reuse: Towards sustainable water management', *Desalination* 156: 181–92.

American Public Health Association (APHA), American Water Works Association (AWWA) and Water Environment Federation (WEF) (1998) *Standard Methods for the Examination of Water and Wastewater*, 20th edn, APHA, Washington D.C.

Burnat, J. (1997) 'On-site wastewater treatment, disposal and re-use: Treatment strategies for the unsewered areas in the West Bank', IHE, Delft, the Netherlands.

Department of Statistics (2002) *Statistical Yearbook*, Jordan.

Dixon, A., Butler, D. and Fewkes, A. (1999a) 'Guidelines for greywater re-use: Health issues', *Journal of the Chartered Institution of Water and Environmental Management (CIWEM)* 13: 322–26.

World Health Organization (WHO) (1989) *Health Guidelines for the Use of Wastewater in Agriculture and Aquaculture* (Technical Report Series 778), WHO, Geneva.

WHO (2000) *Proceedings of the Technical Expert Consultation on Appropriate and Innovative Wastewater Management for Small Communities in EMR Countries*, Eastern Mediterranean Regional Office, Regional Center for Environmental Health Activities, Jordan.

About the authors

Wael Suleiman is a researcher at the Environmental Research Center of the Royal Scientific Society, with focus on wastewater management, treatment, and reuse, bio-solids management and water quality monitoring and assessment. He is a principal researcher in Integrated Wastewater Management Policies and Technologies for Marginal Communities in Jordan, an IDRC-funded project. He is also the project leader in Integrated Graywater Management Policies for Large Water Consumers in Vulnerable Communities of Jordan, an applied research project funded by WADIMENA/IDRC. He holds an MSc in Civil Engineering from the University of Jordan with focus on water and environmental issues. Email: wael@rss.gov.jo

Bassam Al-Hayek is the Director of the Environmental Research Center (ERC) at the Royal Scientific Society.

Moayied Assayed is a researcher at the Environment Research Center of the Royal Scientific Society, and has professional experience in greywater management, risk assessment and water demand management.

Sahar Dalahmeh is Sahar Dalahmeh is an engineer at the Royal Scientific Society.

Nisreen Al-Hmoud is head of water quality studies division at the Energy Research Center.

PART II
Socioeconomic aspects

CHAPTER 5

Stakeholder participation in greywater management in the Jordanian Badia

Sahar Dalahmeh, Moayied Assayed, Wael Suleiman and Bassam Al-Hayek

The aim of this chapter is to illustrate the process of stakeholder participation in greywater (GW) management in the Badia of Jordan. The work was carried out as a part of a project entitled Integrated Wastewater Management Policies and Technologies in Marginal Communities in Jordan, described more fully in Chapter 4. The objectives of the project were to improve the quality of life and well-being for rural Jordanians, strategically support GW use and improve hygienic conditions. The stakeholders participating in GW management included local people, non-governmental organizations (NGOs), community-based organizations (CBOs), governmental authorities and scientists and experts from universities as well as research institutions. Local people were involved in different capacity-building programs, including technical field visits, a participatory rapid (or rural) appraisal (PRA) training course and awareness campaigns. Local people were also involved in data collection, community selection, GW quality and quantity assessment, treatment technology, construction and operation. Experts and governmental authorities participated in treatment technology selection and design. The study revealed that combining the strengths of different stakeholders made up for the scarce learning resources and human and financial resources that are needed to develop GW treatment technology for the Badia region. It was concluded that incorporation of inputs from different stakeholders enhanced the quality, ownership and sustainability of the project.

Introduction

This chapter describes a GW project conducted in the north-eastern Badia of Jordan. Badia is a local term for Jordanian dry lands where the local nomadic and non-nomadic Bedouins live or used to live. The north-eastern Badia of Jordan covers an area of about 25,600 km^2. The population size of the north-eastern Badia was about 28,480 people in 2003, living in 33 small communities. The towns and villages of the Badia are scattered throughout the area and have low-population density (Department of Statistics, 2001).

The existing household sanitation facilities in the Badia were built to satisfy households' demand for privacy and convenience (outdoor toilets and indoor shower rooms). The cultural and religious traditions of Muslim communities of the Badia require the use of water for ablution and washing after defecation, where possible (Al-Jayyousi, 2003).

The current GW use practices in these rural communities include the separation of GW from toilet wastewater (blackwater). Blackwater is generally disposed of in cesspools, and GW (wastewater effluent from the ablution or hand washing basin, kitchen sink, shower room, bath tubs and washing machines) is either used for irrigation or disposed of directly to the environment without treatment (Royal Scientific Society, 2003–06).

The driving forces behind GW separation include religious attitudes and beliefs, the state of the economy and the need to maximize the use of the available water (Al-Jayyousi, 2003; Dutton et al., 1998). According to the teachings of Islam, water containing faeces or urine is considered unclean (*mutanajjis*). Because of this, some people are not content to discharge water from sinks and showers, and kitchen water (i.e. greywater) into the same cesspool as blackwater. In the case of kitchen GW, this also may stem from the fact that it contains some food remains, which are regarded as 'God's gift' (Dutton et al., 1998).

The technicalities of the GW project is more fully described in Chapter 4.

The community involvement in this project included questionnaires, information gathering visits (Pretty and Vodouhê, 1998), and the use of participatory rapid (or rural) appraisal (PRA) (Singh and Rennie, 1996). PRA can be an efficient and cost-effective way of gathering information from local people. PRA techniques rely very much on identifying an overall picture, rather than looking for statistical significance, and emphasize the importance of local knowledge (ibid).

Providing the public with effective means of participation and building trust with communities, by involving them at an early stage in the planning process and in collecting data, assessing needs, building capacity, selecting alternative sites and technologies, and having an input in the management of a project, is a most important tool that ensures the cooperative management of community resources and enhances project quality and sustainability (Ockelford and Reed, 2002).

Sustainable and integrated management of GW in rural communities requires the production of GW appropriate for irrigation without significant negative impacts on health and the environment. Greywater management is directly effected by the awareness of local people and depends on the regular follow-up and maintenance of the treatment facilities by house owners and, in many cases, housewives (Dalahmeh and Assayed, 2007).

The objective of this chapter is to present a case study for the public involvement and participation of different stakeholders in GW management in Jordan.

Research methodology

Preparation

Formal and informal information meetings were held with community leaders and representatives, municipality directors, principals of girls' and boys' schools, and representatives of non-governmental organizations (NGOs) and community-based organizations (CBOs) to introduce the project idea, objectives, methodology of work, and role of the community in GW management. A local stakeholder committee (LSC) was formed by the community itself. The committee was comprised of 15 people (4 women and 11 men) from different communities in the project area.

Professional officers from the relevant government authorities, experts and scientists from research centres, and academic institutions in Jordan were invited to participate in the project through steering and expert committees.

Capacity building

A four-day training course on participatory development communication (PDC) and PRA was organized by the research team and delivered by CARE International in Jordan/CARE Australia and PLAN:NET, Canada. The training targeted the LSC members and was held in the Um Al Quttain Social Club. Indicators were selected to measure the effectiveness in capacity building. These were: 1) number of participants; 2) training reports prepared by the trainers; 3) participants' knowledge about PRA methods before and after training.

Five field trips to wastewater and GW treatment-and-use projects in Jordan were organized for the LSC and other community representatives. The indicators used to measure the effectiveness of technical visits in increasing people's knowledge of wastewater issues were: 1) the number of participants; 2) field reports prepared by the trainees; 3) participants knowledge about wastewater and GW before and after trips.

An environmental awareness campaign was launched by the Environment and Economic Investment Cooperative Society (one of the NGOs working on relevant fields in the project area). The awareness campaign targeted community leaders, religious leaders, housewives, school teachers, school students and public health specialists. The awareness campaigns included three main activities: scoping sessions, best environmental drawing contest and lectures and workshops. The indicators used to measure the effectiveness of environmental awareness campaigns were: 1) the number and types of target groups; 2) mission report of the Environment and Economic Investment Cooperative Society; 3) participants' knowledge about GW management before and after the awareness campaigns.

Data collection and situation analysis

The research team and LSC collected social, economic, environmental and technical data relating to wastewater and GW in the study area using PRA tools and methods. Data was collected from a sample of 8–15 per cent of the population by five work teams, each consisting of three to five members including at least one woman. A total of 404 household-level interviews were carried out during 13 days of field work in 33 communities.

Greywater quantities in six households were measured by one community member on a daily basis. Physical and chemical parameters of GW were analysed in the laboratories of an environmental research centre. Expert and steering committees participated in assessing the quality of GW generated in the study area based on the Jordanian wastewater guidelines and standards of use (see Chapter 4 for more details).

Community selection criteria and treatment technology criteria

Community selection criteria were set by the research team and LSC to identify the best communities within the project area where pilot field experiments for GW collection, treatment, and use could be conducted.

The expert committee and steering committee then developed GWT selection criteria. The criteria took into consideration GW characteristics, environmental requirements, social and economic requirements and standards and regulations for use. Five treatment technologies were proposed to treat GW in the study area, and they were evaluated in view of the criteria. The technologies included septic tank, sand filter, constructed wetlands, sequential batch reactor and up-flow anaerobic sludge blanket (UASB).

Design criteria were developed by the expert committee and research team to design the selected treatment systems (see Chapter 4).

Construction and operation of treatment systems

A septic tank followed by an intermittent sand filter was constructed in Abu Al-Farth Village, and a UASB was constructed near Zamlat Al-Amir Ghazi Village. A training session on the construction and operational requirement of the treatment systems was held, targeting house owners and other local people in the villages. The flow of information between the different stakeholders of the project is shown in Figure 5.1.

Results and discussion

Preparation

Over a four-day period 15 information meetings were attended by about 150 participants including community leaders, community members, officials, NGOs and CBOs in the study area. The meetings enabled the project team to

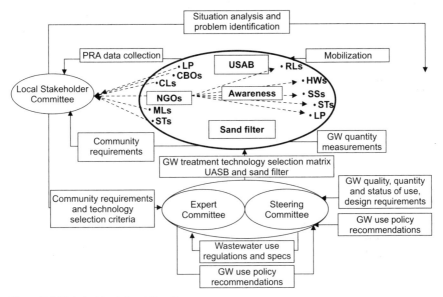

Figure 5.1 Stakeholder information flow

introduce the project objectives, activities, and anticipated outcomes to the communities. Thirty questions and remarks on wastewater-related issues were raised by the audience. The meetings were the main tool used to facilitate dialogue over GW-management issues and provided an opportunity for the interaction of communities with the existing water and wastewater issues in Jordan.

An LSC consisting of 15 people (11 men and 4 women) from the study area was formed. During a 44-month period, more than 50 regular meetings were held between researchers and the LSC to discuss the implementation of activities of the project and define the roles and tasks of the LSC in the project. The LSC brought together the views and opinions of the local people with other stakeholders, such as the project team, government authorities, and research institutions.

A steering committee of seven members from the Ministry of Water and Irrigation, Ministry of Health, Ministry of Environment, Badia Research and Development Center, and the LSC was formed. The role of the committee was to discuss different aspects of GW management in the rural communities, future governmental plans, and strategies for the development of integrated management of the Badia resources.

An expert committee was formulated and consisted of 10 scientists and experts from the Royal Scientific Society, University of Jordan, Jordan University for Science and Technology, National Center for Agricultural Research and Technology Transfer, Ministry of Water and Irrigation, and Inter-Islamic Network on Water Resources Development and Management (INWRDAM). The role of this committee was to establish a network for discussion, assessment, and evaluation of, as well as exchange of information about, affordable and attractive GW treatment options that suit the study area.

Capacity building

One major challenge concerning community involvement in GW projects in rural areas in Jordan was the development of community knowledge about GW-related issues. The levels of understanding and knowledge about GW management and use were increased through awareness campaigns, site visits, training courses, workshops, regular meetings, and group discussions, all of which were among the activities of the project.

About 30 community members participated in a PRA training course. The course enabled the LSC to conduct face-to-face interviews, semi-structured interviews, community mapping, daily routine, observations, and data analysis during the data collection phase and led to identifying technical, political, social and financial issues, problems and constraints currently facing wastewater management in small communities.

Five rounds of field trips were organized for community members (see Chapter 4 for details of these field trips). These visits had a positive impact on the communities' perspectives and perceptions of GW treatment and use, and further developed community know-how and provided an opportunity to be exposed to other experiences and practices in GW management.

About 500 school students, 35 school teachers, 15 religious leaders, 50 housewives, and 8 health inspectors participated in the awareness lectures and workshops that targeted the study area. There was a drawing contest which 230 school students participated in and a poster for the best seven environmental drawings was designed, published and distributed among schools, NGOs, CBOs and local people.

Evaluation of the awareness campaigns shows that there was an increase in people's knowledge of methods and practices that could be used to help improve the quality of the GW at source, usage of treated GW and health impacts of direct contact with untreated GW. The awareness campaigns helped the target groups to understand the role of local people in managing GW resources, the role of religious leaders in encouraging appropriate water conservation and use conditions, and the role of teachers in disseminating information about GW management to their students who can transfer the new knowledge to their families.

CBOs and NGOs played an important role in capacity building and information dissemination. This was accomplished through the participation of the Anakeed Al Khair Society, the Um Al Quttain Social Club, and the Environmental and Economic Investment Society in hosting PRA training, organizing the awareness workshops, presenting lectures, and distributing posters.

Data collection and situation analysis

Local people participated thoroughly in data collection and situation analysis during the initial phase of the project. The following issues were identified by the LSC during the PRA and socioeconomic surveys:

- The project area suffers from a water shortage problem. Domestic water is supplied through the public network for only 24 hours each week. Inhabitants purchase water from the private sector (water tankers) particularly in the summer period. People spend five per cent of their income on the water bill.
- The community relies mainly on unlined cesspools as on-site wastewater collection systems. In some areas, cesspools are rarely emptied. In others, the cesspools are pumped out on a monthly basis, at an average cost of JOD21 per pump-out (based on exchange rates of May 2009, JOD1 = US$1.41). The closest legal liquid waste disposal site is 80 km away from the area, and inhabitants believe that the wastewater pumped out of cesspools is being illegally disposed of in nearby streams. About 62 per cent of the public in the project area utilize pit latrines or ventilated improved pit latrines, 33 per cent have a traditional (no-flush) indoor toilet, while only 1 per cent use flush toilet (compared to 89 per cent on the national level). Only 40 per cent of the community has showers and kitchen sinks.
- Two-thirds of the community separate GW from blackwater, apparently mainly for religious considerations. Greywater is being used directly (without any treatment) to irrigate the planted backyards in an uncontrolled manner, paying little attention to health aspects.
- The majority of the rural communities of the Badia region are aware of the existence of GW problems that affect both public health and the environment. The major public health issues attributed to GW are those related to the presence of insects, rodents and offensive odours.
- Most people show acceptance to the idea of treating GW on a household level and reusing it for the irrigation of fodder or olive trees. People have willingness to operate and maintain GW treatment facilities.

Community selection and treatment technology selection and design criteria

Community selection criteria were developed by the LSC and research team and are described in the chapter by Suleiman and others in this volume.

Based on these criteria, Abu Al-Farth (Rawdat Al-Amir Ali) Village and a nearby settlement near Zamlat Al-Amir Ghazi were selected to implement treatment units in their territories.

The participation of the expert committee, the steering committee and the research team resulted in developing treatment technology evaluation and design criteria. The evaluation criteria are shown in Table 5.1.

Table 5.1 Treatment technology evaluation criteria

Source characteristics	Community requirements	Receiving environment	Use opportunity and local regulations
Effectiveness in handling high organic loads (Yes/No) Effectiveness in removing BOD, TSS, FOG, N, and pathogens removal efficiency (%) Ability to operate under variable flow patterns, shock loads (Yes/No)	Land requirement Area (m2) Production of odours (Yes/No) Maintenance requirement (Daily, Weekly, Monthly, Yearly) (Yes/No, type maintenance required, cost) Operation requirements, is it a user-friendly system? (Yes/No) Approximate construction costs (JOD) Approximate operation costs (JOD)	Need for specific environmental conditions (temperature, topography) (Yes/No) Availability of construction materials/treatment media in the study area (Yes/No)	Effluent quality meets the Jordanian Specification 893/2002 for Restricted Irrigation (JSIM, 2002) (Yes/No) Losses (evaporation, evapo-transpiration) (High/Low)

Five treatment options were evaluated using the above-mentioned treatment technology criteria. These options include: 1) septic tank; 2) intermittent sand filters; 3) wetlands; 4) sequencing batch reactor; 5) up-flow anaerobic sludge blanket (UASB).

Out of the five systems, the UASB and septic tank followed by intermittent sand filter were selected by the expert and steering committees to be designed and constructed in the study area. The septic tank–sand filter and UASB units were designed based on the criteria in Table 5.2, which were also set by the expert and steering committees taking into consideration the acceptance of the house owners.

The participation of local people was greatest in the short-term data collection, situation analysis and community selection phase, and long-term

Table 5.2 Design criteria for the treatment systems

Household owner	MM	FA
Village	Abu Al-Farth (Rawdat Al-Amir Ali)	Nayifa (near Zamlat Al-Amir Ghazi)
Treatment option	Septic tank followed by intermittent sand filter	Up-flow anaerobic sludge blanket (UASB)
Design flow	150 litre/day	300 litre/day
Design BOD$_5$/COD	BOD5: 1,000 mg/l	COD: 2,500 mg/l
Design TSS	750 mg/l	780 mg/l

implementation and operation phase. The communities were not so involved in the design phase, since they were deemed not to have the necessary engineering skills. The communities, through the LSC, participated in deciding the type of the treatment technology that best suited their social and economic conditions.

Construction and operation of treatment units

Septic tanks followed by intermittent sand filters were constructed in single households in Abu Al-Farth Village (Rawdat Al-Amir Ali). A UASB unit was constructed near Zamlat Al-Amir Ghazi Village.

The units were built by the communities themselves using local construction materials, fittings, and machinery available in the area. The treatment units were operated and maintained by the households.

The sustainability of treatment units was strengthened by conducting training sessions on construction and operational requirements of the treatment systems. The training was targeted at householders and other interested people in the villages. Arabic-language guidelines, *Guidelines for Greywater Management on Household Level in the Small Communities in Northeastern Badia of Jordan*, were prepared by the research team in consultation with the steering committee, the expert committee, and LSC. The guidelines were distributed to the people in the study area.

Conclusion

Integrated management of GW in the Badia of Jordan is a challenge because of the local traditions and values held by the communities. Nonetheless, GW use as a means of increasing the availability of affordable water is of great importance to the improvement of the quality of life for such marginalized communities. Its successful implementation was seen to hinge on early involvement of the communities in the selection, design, implementation, operation, and maintenance of the treatment systems in ways that suited local environmental conditions and socioeconomic circumstances.

It was seen that the existing knowledge of local people should be recognized, and participatory approaches should be applied when investigating integrated water resource management programs for small communities. However, this was usefully combined with intensive awareness campaigns. Field visits of local people to other wastewater treatment and use projects were seen to be valuable in terms of developing community knowledge and sharing knowledge and ideas.

Combining the knowledge and experience of the different stakeholders (local communities, governmental organizations, and experts) was seen to increase the available human resource base, especially in a rural, semi-isolated region like the Badia.

The development of a common understanding between local communities and the various responsible governmental agencies is considered an important requirement to encourage taking responsibility and provide the users with the support and knowledge they need. This approach makes the project more likely to be sustainable.

Acknowledgments

The authors would like to express their deep gratitude to the International Development Research Centre (IDRC), Canada, for the financial support they provided to the Environmental Research Center to implement the project Integrated Wastewater Management Policies and Technologies in the Marginal Communities in Jordan, in which different types of stakeholder participation were explored. Special thanks go to Dr Lamia Al Fattal from IDRC, Mrs Samira Smirat from PLAN:NET Ltd, the local stakeholder committee, the steering committee, the expert committee, Um Al Quttain Social Club, Anakeed Al Khair Society and the Environmental and Economic Investment Society for their cooperation and continuous support.

References

Al-Jayyousi, O.R. (2003) 'Greywater reuse: towards sustainable water management', *Desalination* 156: 181–92.
Dalahmeh S. and Assayed, M.K. (2007) *Guidelines for greywater management on household level in the small communities in the northeastern Badia of Jordan*, Royal Scientific Society, Amman and IDRC, Canada.
Department of Statistics (2001) *Statistical Yearbook*. Jordan
Dutton, R., Clarke, J.I. and Battikhi, A. (1998) *Arid Land Resources and Their Management: Jordan's Desert Margin*, Kegan Paul International, New York.
Jordanian Institute for Standards and Metrology (JSIM) (2002) *Jordan Standard, No 893.2002*.
Ockelford, J. and Reed, B. (2002) *Participatory Planning for Integrated Rural Water Supply and Sanitation Programmes: Guidelines and Manual*, Water, Engineering and Development Centre, Loughborough University, England.
Pretty, J. and Vodouhê, S.D. (1998) 'Using rapid or participatory rural appraisal', in B.E. Swanson, R.P. Bentz and A.J. Sofranko (eds), *Improving Agricultural Extension: A Reference Manual*, Food and Agriculture Organisation of the United Nations, Rome.
Royal Scientific Society (2003–2006) 'Integrated wastewater management policies and technologies in the marginal communities of Jordan' [technical reports], Amman.
Singh, N. and Rennie, J.K. (1996) *Participatory Research for Sustainable Livelihoods: A Guidebook for Field Projects on Adaptive Strategies*, International Institute for Sustainable Development, Canada.

About the authors

Sahar Dalahmeh is a mid-career engineer who has worked at the Royal Scientific Society on several projects in the fields of water resources, wastewater, and GW management. She holds an MSc in Water Resources and Environment. She has experience in community participation and development in water and wastewater fields.
Email: sahar@rss.gov.jo

Moayied Assayed is a researcher at the Environment Research Center of the Royal Scientific Society.

Wael Suleiman is a researcher at the Environmental Research Center of the Royal Scientific Society.

Bassam Al-Hayek is the Director of the Environmental Research Center (ERC) at the Royal Scientific Society.

CHAPTER 6
Comparative socioeconomic study of greywater and cesspit systems in Ramallah, Palestine

Maher Abu-Madi, Rashed Al-Sa'ed, Nidal Mahmoud and Jamal Burnat

Palestinian rural and peri-urban communities represent more than 60 per cent of the total population but lack appropriate management of their wastewater. While most rural households are internally equipped with proper sanitation facilities, there is a problem with the way wastewater is discharged. Traditional cesspits are used for the collection of excreta, which often percolates into the surrounding soil and jeopardizes groundwater aquifers. Several non-governmental organizations (NGOs) promote on-site sanitation for rural communities with emphasis on separation of blackwater and greywater (GW) and utilizing treated GW in garden irrigation. However, the implementation of GW systems is often limited by the availability of external funding, and most Palestinian communities have not reached a stage where they are able to implement GW systems with their own funding.

This chapter studies the social and economic feasibility of existing GW systems and the public perceptions towards them in Western Ramallah villages. The researchers surveyed 30 households that use GW systems and 100 households that use traditional cesspits.

Introduction

The Occupied Palestinian Territories are facing a rapid population growth against a context of limited water-resources and poor wastewater management. The Palestinian rural and peri-urban communities represent more than 60 per cent of the total population. Most Palestinian households are internally equipped with proper sanitation facilities (plumbed toilets, sinks, drains, etc.), but lack means for proper collection and discharge. Only around 25 per cent of Palestinian households (35 per cent of the total population) are served by central sewerage systems, and a further 17 per cent of the collected municipal wastewater (from 6 per cent of the population) is partially treated (Abu-Madi et al., 2000; Mahmoud et al., 2003). The high percentage of unsewered areas and lack of treatment plants cause an over-reliance on traditional on-site systems for wastewater disposal, mainly cesspits and septic tanks.[1] Traditionally, each household has a cesspit for the collection of excreta, which often percolates into the surrounding soil. This is a disposal system fraught with disadvantages, since it jeopardizes groundwater and the environment (Plancenter, 1997). In addition, when the surrounding soil becomes saturated, cesspits require frequent emptying using expensive private tankers. Cesspit emptying is costly and disruptive and often causes additional environmental pollution. When cesspits become full, an unpleasant odour spreads around the area. The odour problems are exacerbated when the cesspits are emptied and often cause complaints from neighbours. Also, tanker operators who empty the cesspits often do not follow rules and regulations and discharge the emptied septage within the surroundings of the communities, especially in agricultural areas and open fields.

Substantial efforts have been made by Palestinian governmental and non-governmental institutions to improve sanitation services through centralized (off-site) and on-site wastewater treatment facilities. Nevertheless, the following major challenges are reflective of the current sanitation situation:

- The low-population densities and spatial expansion in rural and peri-urban communities, and the long distances from potential centralized wastewater disposal systems often mean that economies of scale do not exist. Therefore, centralized systems for wastewater collection and disposal require disproportionately large investments which are unaffordable to the majority of the rural and peri-urban poor (UN, 2001; Parkinson and Tayler, 2003).
- Limited funding is a major obstacle for the development and maintenance of water and wastewater services. Current wastewater treatment facilities are heavily overloaded, have inadequate maintenance and are of low cost recovery (World Bank, 2004; Al-Sa'ed, 2006).
- Some side effects of the Israeli occupation hinder the construction of wastewater treatment plants by Palestinians. These include imposing stringent effluent quality-standards and requiring the connection of Israeli settlements to Palestinian treatment plants. The Palestinian institutions, therefore, try to adopt on-site solutions that are environmentally-sound and opt for the treatment and use of household wastewater. Because of this, there is increasing interest in the separation of blackwater (toilet wastewater) and GW and the use of reclaimed GW in garden irrigation.

Greywater projects implemented in similar arid and semi-arid countries revealed that the use of treated GW in agricultural irrigation is a technically feasible and economically affordable alternative in several case studies. Jamrah and colleagues (2004) investigated the Omanis' perceptions towards the use of treated GW and found that about 82 per cent of respondents were in favour of GW treatment and use in agricultural irrigation. Nevertheless, Prathapar and colleagues (2005) identified several constraints for the application of GW systems in Oman, related to concerns over effluent quality and institutional, legal, financial, and social constraints. Greywater treatment and use within household irrigation projects implemented in Jordan showed reasonable ratios of benefits to costs ranging from 2.8 to 9.4 (Faruqui and Al-Jayyousi, 2002).

In general, water and wastewater services in the Palestinian urban and rural communities are characterized by poor cost recovery, where sustainability can only be maintained through external funding. The majority of implemented greywater systems (GWS) in the West Bank have been technically and financially supported by NGOs (e.g. PHG, PARC and PWEG) and aid agencies (e.g. IDRC, ACDI-VOCA, DFID and SC). Nevertheless, the rural and peri-urban communities have still not reached a stage where they can replicate such systems with their own funding. Many GW treatment-and-use projects failed, where planning, design, and implementation were based mainly on technical aspects, without adequate examination of the economic or socio-cultural issues. Therefore, a socio-cultural, ecological and cost–benefit analysis should be considered to ensure that on-site GW treatment-and-use schemes are designed to be sustainable, irrespective of the project size.

The development and performance of different treatment technologies and effluent-use schemes have been addressed by most past research efforts, whereas the socioeconomic aspects of GW use have been insufficiently tackled (Al-Sa'ed, 2000; Ogoshi et al., 2001; Dallas et al., 2004; Friedler and Hadari, 2005; Friedler et al., 2005). The lack of comparative studies on GW and traditional systems for domestic wastewater management and safe effluent disposal prompted this research study.

Objectives

The main aim of this study was to compare the socioeconomics of GWS and common cesspits in five Western Ramallah rural and peri-urban communities: Bil'in, Deir Ibzi', Kafr Ni'ma, Kharbatha Bani Harith, and Ras Karkar. The specific objectives were to assess and compare the direct costs and benefits of existing GWS and traditional cesspits and to better understand the public perceptions towards GWS and use of treated GW in irrigated agriculture.

Methodology

Field visits and a questionnaire survey were conducted in 2006 in Western Ramallah towns and villages. The total sample size was 130 households of which 30 had already constructed GWS while the other 100 relied on cesspits for disposal of their wastewater. The type of GWS observed in this study is the 'septic tank–up-flow gravel filter' (Burnat and Mahmoud, 2004). The owners of the GWS in each of the five villages had been pre-identified and selected for the survey. The households with cesspits had been randomly selected and equally distributed between the five villages with 20 cesspits in each. The questionnaires included sections about the interviewee, household, water, sanitation, land use and perceptions. The SPSS statistical program and excel spreadsheets were used for data manipulation and analysis. The original cost data was collected in the local currency (Israeli new sheqel) and converted to US dollars at a 2006 rate of US$1 = ILS4.3.

The cost calculations comprised investment/capital costs (CAPEX) and recurring/operational costs (OPEX). In addition to a separate cesspit for the blackwater, CAPEX covered the costs associated with excavation, construction, piping, pumps and labour. OPEX covered costs associated with electricity, labour, and emptying/de-sludging, sampling, checking and cleaning. Obviously, these costs varied according to the number of people served by each system. The financial valuation of GWS and cesspit systems was based upon the direct benefits and costs to households – mainly the water and sanitation expenditures. Lack of data prevented the researchers from assessing the indirect benefits and costs of both systems in relation to health, environmental and agronomic impacts. The benefit–cost ratio of GWS was calculated based upon the net present value of the total costs and benefits (Abu-Madi, 2006).

The contingent valuation method was used to elicit households' willingness to have a GWS as well as their willingness to use the produced effluent for garden irrigation, and to identify the reasons behind public decisions towards GWS and their effluent use (Abu-Madi et al., 2003; Hussain et al., 2001; Po et al., 2005).

Results and discussion

Construction cost (CAPEX) comparison of GWS and cesspits

Table 6.1 shows the capital cost (CAPEX) data. The average CAPEX of the surveyed GWS and cesspits was US$1,212/household and US$1,405/household, respectively. The per capita CAPEX was within the range US$49–388/person (with an average of US$250/person) and US$74–581/person (with an average of US$180/person), for GWS and cesspits respectively. The costs varied between households even where the same types of GWS were used. These variations are attributed to: 1) variations in family size; 2) differences in the types of cesspits/tanks (three different types were noted); 3) variation in the excavation costs from one site to another due to different soil types; 4) modifications made by some households to their existing cesspits; 5) the use of family members and friends for construction labour; 6) the use of locally available materials; 7) the approximations made by some interviewees, some of whom were not directly involved in the construction. It is worth mentioning that households who had already invested in constructing cesspits would have to bear additional financial burden if they decided to shift to GWS.

Table 6.1 CAPEX comparison of GWS and cesspits

CAPEX	N*	Minimum	Maximum	Mean	Std. deviation
GWS					
US$	30	488.4	2,325.6	1,212.4	527.1
US$/person	30	48.8	387.6	179.9	82.6
Cesspits					
US$	100	465.1	3,604.7	1,405.1	611.4
US$/person	100	74.0	581.4	249.5	102.3

* N = number of households

Operation and maintenance costs (OPEX) comparison of GWS and cesspits

Table 6.2 shows the operational expenditure (OPEX). These results show that operating and maintaining the GWS was cheaper than maintaining the cesspits. The OPEX of the surveyed GWS varied between US$23.3 and US$139.5/year (an average of US$65.7). The OPEX of the 37 cesspits that were emptied frequently was within the range of US$23.3–976.7/year (an average of US$151.6/year). The reason for this high variation is attributed to differences in the frequency of cesspit emptying, which ranged from 1 to 24 times per year (with a mean value of 6 times per year). This range depended on the cesspit type and volume as well as the permeability of the surrounding soil. The other 63 cesspits were not emptied, thus no operational costs were incurred. However, our cost comparison did not consider this as an option since it is not environmentally acceptable.

Benefits of GWS

Table 6.3 illustrates the household expenditure on water during the study. Although no 'before-system' data is available, it can be provisionally inferred that one likely direct benefit of using GWS was the saving in the water bill, i.e., saving in potable water consumption as a result of substituting potable water

Table 6.2 OPEX comparison of GWS and cesspits per household unit

OPEX	N*	Minimum	Maximum	Mean	Std. deviation
GWS					
US$/year	30	23.3	139.5	65.7	26.2
US$/person/year	30	2.9	29.1	9.9	5.0
Cesspits					
US$/year	37**	23.3	976.7	151.6	206.4
US$/person/year	37**	2.6	203.5	25.2	38.8

* N = number of households
** Number of cesspits that are emptied at least once a year

Table 6.3 Impact of GWS and cesspits on households' expenditure on water and wastewater

	N*	Minimum	Maximum	Mean	Std. deviation
GWS					
Water expenditure (US$/month)	30	11.63	58.14	28.64	12.73
Water expenditure (US$/person/month)	30	1.94	11.63	4.22	2.17
Water expenditure (% of income)	30	1.25	18.00	6.48	3.90
Wastewater expenditure (% of income)	30	0.14	1.33	0.54	0.32
Cesspits					
Water expenditure (US$/month)	100	11.63	93.02	38.86	23.19
Water expenditure (US$/person/month)	100	1.45	23.26	7.24	5.39
Water expenditure (% of income)	100	1.14	35.00	8.47	6.94
Wastewater expenditure (% of income)	37**	0.33	8.75	2.29	2.28

* N = number of households
** Number of the cesspits that are emptied at least once a year

with GW for irrigation purposes. The results of the study showed that the households' average expenditure on water supply was about US$28.6/month (US$4.2/person/month) and US$38.9/month (US$7.2/person/month) in the cases of GWS and cesspits, respectively. The average share of the water supply expenditure as a percentage of the households' income was lower for GWS users (6.5 per cent and 8.5 per cent for GWS and cesspit cases, respectively). The results also showed that the average share of sanitation expenditure as a percentage of the households' income was lower for GWS users (about 0.5 per cent and 2.3 per cent for GWS and cesspit users, respectively). These figures could be considered high when compared with the international affordability level (4 per cent of the annual income) for water supply, and wastewater services (DANCEE, 2002; World Bank, 2004). However, the figure for GWS (about 7 per cent) is lower than that for cesspits (about 11 per cent).

Benefit–cost ratio of GWS

The direct benefit–cost ratio of GWS was calculated based on the net present value (NPV) of total costs and benefits according to the equations listed below, taken from Abu-Madi, (2006). The following assumptions were made:

- discount rate of 7 per cent;
- life time of the GWS is 30 years;
- constant annual OPEX and constant annual water saving;
- 70 per cent of the households' total water supply that enters the GWS and used in garden irrigation;
- annual benefits (B) = annual value of water saving + annual avoided cost of cesspit emptying;
- value of each cubic meter of reused water is US$1;
- avoided cost of cesspit emptying is US$150/year/household.

$$NPV = C/(1+i)^n \tag{6.1}$$
$$NPV = C_1/(1+i) + C_2/(1+i)^2 + C_3/(1+i)^3 + \ldots + C_n/(1+i)^n \tag{6.2}$$

In case of equal annual operation and maintenance costs
(i.e., $C_1 = C_2 = C_3 = \ldots = C_n = C$), a simple equation for NPV is derived:

$$NPV = C . \sum_{t=0}^{n} [1/(1+i)^t]$$

or

$$NPV_{OPEX} = OPEX \cdot \{1-(1+i)^{-n}\}/i \tag{6.4}$$
$$NPV_{TOTEX} = CAPEX + NPV_{OPEX} \tag{6.5}$$
$$NPV_{Benefits} = B \cdot \{1-(1+i)^{-n}\}/i \tag{6.6}$$
$$B/C \text{ ratio} = NPV_{Benefits} / NPV_{TOTEX} \tag{6.7}$$

The net present value benefit–cost ratio analysis for the studied GWS is shown in Table 6.4. This analysis shows that the direct benefit–cost ratio ranges between 1.2 and 4.2 (mean 2.2). These results support the findings published earlier by Faruqui and Al-Jayyousi (2002) on benefit–cost ratios of Jordanian GW use in agricultural irrigation ranging from 2.8 to 9.4. The results show that the direct benefits of using GWS were high even before considering the indirect benefits associated with preventing groundwater pollution, safeguarding public health, and the nutrient-rich irrigation water.

Public perceptions towards GWS and use of reclaimed greywater

Despite their high cost cesspits are often constructed by rural households with the household's own funds. On the other hand, the available GWS were mainly constructed with external funding, except for a very few cases. One of the study objectives was, therefore, to better understand this phenomenon, by examining public perceptions of the establishment of GWS with and without external funding. The results showed that about 72 per cent of the surveyed households were willing to implement GWS with external funding while 17 per cent would be willing to fund a GWS themselves. These results were in harmony with the findings of other research studies in the same study area. A study by Al-Sa'ed (in press) conducted on the socioeconomic aspects of decentralized sanitation in

Table 6.4 Benefit–cost ratio of GWS

	Capita per house	CAPEX (US$)	Annual OPEX (US$/yr)	NPV of total OPEX (US$)	NPV TOTEX (US$)	Annual benefits (US$ yr)	NPV of total benefits (US$)	Benefit–cost ratio
Mean	7.1	1,212.4	65.7	815.7	2,028.1	331.4	4,112.4	2.2
Minimum	4.0	488.4	23.3	288.6	1,088.8	252.2	3,129.6	1.2
Maximum	11.0	2,325.6	139.5	1,731.5	3,335.6	431.1	5,348.9	4.2
Std. deviation*	1.9	527.1	26.2	324.7	622.1	48.1	596.6	0.8

* Number of GWS = 30

small Palestinian communities revealed that about 60 per cent of people were unwilling to consider small on-site sanitation systems. The major reason behind these findings was that most (80 per cent) of the respondents did not show a willingness to pay or contribute to the construction costs. Another study by Al-Sa'ed and Mubarak (2006) showed that more than 50 per cent of the respondents in Ramallah and Al-Bireh district were against having new on-site treatment systems and favoured centralized wastewater collection and treatment options, while only 18 per cent showed a willingness to contribute partially to the construction costs. Published data on public attitudes towards GW use in Oman supports these results (Jamrah et al., 2004).

From the survey of 83 households in Western Ramallah villages, it appears that the major reasons behind the resistance to self-fund the implementation of GWS were:

- unwillingness to restructure their internal piping systems in order to separate blackwater from GW (53 per cent);
- unwillingness to use the reclaimed GW for garden irrigation (33 per cent);
- belief in the availability of external funding for GWS (21 per cent);
- inability to afford the construction costs (17 per cent).

For those households who were unwilling to implement GWS even with external funding, (28 households), the reasons stated were:

- satisfaction with their existing cesspits that required no emptying (90 per cent);
- unwillingness to use reclaimed GW for garden irrigation (86 per cent);
- unwillingness to restructure their internal piping systems in order to separate blackwater from GW (63 per cent).

It is worth noting that health risks were not a feature of the replies, and that the literature reports that there are no recorded cases of anyone falling ill as a result of household recycling of GW (Marshall, 1996; Baker and Jean, 2000), although more work needs to be done on health risks.

Conclusion

This work, though based on a small sample size, indicates that GW systems are superior to traditional cesspits in terms of: 1) construction costs; 2) operation and maintenance costs; 3) contribution to households' water consumption and expenditure reduction. In addition, the ratio of direct benefits to costs of GWS is high even without considering the indirect benefits. Nevertheless, the public perceptions were positive only towards externally-funded GWS and negative towards self-funded ones. The negative perceptions were attributed to: 1) refusal to restructure their internal piping systems to separate blackwater from GW; 2) refusal to use the reclaimed GW in garden irrigation; 3) availability of external funding; 4) unaffordable construction costs.

Under the prevailing conditions of the Israeli occupation and restrictions on the implementation of centralized wastewater treatment plants, GW treatment and use could be a potential partial solution for water shortage and wastewater-associated problems in Palestinian rural and peri-urban areas. The Palestinian Water Authority should consider developing, in cooperation with relevant institutions, strategies and standards that encourage GW treatment and use while limiting the application of cesspits.

Greywater development projects in the study area are characterized by an over-reliance on donor funding, despite the widespread willingness to self-fund traditional cesspits and septic tanks. This suggests that there is an awareness gap about the virtues of GWS and the drawbacks of cesspits. More efforts are, therefore, needed by the local and international concerned institutions to change these perceptions through participatory awareness campaigns that would make use of the existing GWS as demonstration sites. Donors also should consider providing technical and financial support only to poor families and providing only technical assistance to those who are willing to fund GWS themselves.

The implementation of GWS is more likely to be successful in new premises where separation of blackwater from GW is technically feasible. The use of GWS would be further encouraged by integrating GWS requirements in the national building codes and by aiming at effective promotion of legal GW use on a large scale. However, before GWS can become a common feature in residential buildings, more field testing is essential to ensure safe treatment and use practices.

More research is needed on the economics of the existing GW treatment-and-use systems in Palestine and other countries of the region.

Notes

[1]   Traditional cesspits were excavations in the ground, preferably (from the households' perspective) in permeable soils to reduce emptying costs. This system is still common in rural areas that are not controlled by local authorities. In peri-urban and urban communities, another system – the septic tank – is applied. This consists of an excavation in the ground with concrete walls on all sides, except for the base which is left permeable. The wastewater (combined) discharged into these two systems might therefore reach the groundwater. The environmentally-sound cesspit/septic tank approach which is now required by the Palestinian Authority must be confined and impermeable to avoid infiltration of pollutants to the surrounding soil and the aquifer. This type of system implies frequent emptying from residents at costs higher than they can afford. Typical volumes of the three types of cesspits/tanks vary between 20 to 60 m^3.

References

Abu-Madi, M. (2006) 'Political economy for environmental planners' [lecture notes WEEN630], MSc Programs, Faculty of Graduate Studies, Birzeit University, Palestine.

Abu-Madi, M., Al-Sa'ed, R., Braadbart, O. and Alaerts, G. (2000) 'Selection criteria for appropriate sanitation in the Palestinian rural and semi-urban communities', *The International Symposium on Water Sector Capacity Building and Research in Palestine*, Birzeit University, Birzeit, West Bank.

Abu-Madi, M., Braadbart, O., Al-Sa'ed, R. and Alaerts, G. (2003) 'Willingness of farmers to pay for reclaimed wastewater in Jordan and Tunisia', *Water Science and Technology: Water Supply* 3: 115–22.

Al-Sa'ed, R. (2000) 'Wastewater management for small communities in Palestine', *The Technical Expert Consultation on Appropriate and Innovative Wastewater Management for Small Communities in EMR Countries*, Centre for Environmental Health Activities (CEHA), World Health Organization (WHO), Amman, Jordan.

Al-Sa'ed, R. (2006) 'Technical and socio-cultural assessment of urban and rural wastewater treatment facilities in Palestine', MSc Report, Institute of Environmental and Water Studies, Birzeit University, Palestine.

Al-Sa'ed, R. and Mubarak, S. (2006) 'Sustainability assessment of onsite sanitation facilities in Ramallah-Albireh district with emphasis on technical, socio-cultural and financial aspects', *International Journal of Management of Environmental Quality* 17: 140–56.

Barker, A. and Jean, E. (2000) 'Recycling gray water for home gardens' [online], University of Massachusetts Cooperative Extension Service, Amherst, MA, available from: http://umassgreeninfo.org/fact_sheets/plant_culture/gray_water_for_gardens.html [accessed 18 January 2009].

Burnat, J. and Mahmoud, N. (2004) 'Evaluation of on-site grey wastewater treatment plants performance in Bilien and Biet-Diko villages, Palestine', *Bridging the Gap Conference*, Dead Sea, Jordan.

Dallas, S., Scheffe, B. and Ho, G. (2004) 'Reedbeds for greywater treatment – case study in Santa Elena-Monteverde, Costa Rica, Central America', *Ecological Engineering* 23: 55–61.

Danish Cooperation for Environment in Eastern Europe (DANCEE) (2002) *Water Prices in CEE and CIS Countries: A Toolkit for Assessing Willingness to Pay, Affordability and Political Acceptability* (vol. I), DANCEE, Ministry of the Environment, Copenhagen.

Faruqui, N. and Al-Jayyousi, O. (2002) 'Greywater reuse in urban agriculture for poverty alleviation', *Water International* 27: 387–94.

Friedler, E., Galil, N. and Kovalio, R. (2005) 'On-site greywater treatment and reuse in multi-storey buildings', *Water Science and Technology* 51: 187–94.

Friedler, E. and Hadari, M. (2005) 'Economic feasibility of on-site greywater reuse in multi-storey buildings', *Desalination* 190: 221–34.

Hussain, I., Raschid, L., Hanjra, M., Marikar, F. and Hoek, W. (2001) 'A Framework for analyzing socioeconomic, health and environmental impacts of wastewater use in agriculture in developing countries' [online], available from http://www.lk.iwmi.org/pubs/working/WOR26.pdf [accessed 15 October 2006].

Jamrah, A., Al-Futaisi, A., Prathapar, S., Ahmad, M. and Al Harasi, A. (2004) 'Evaluating greywater reuse potential for sustainable water resources management in the Sultanate of Oman', *The International Conference on Water Demand Management*, Dead Sea, Jordan.

Mahmoud, N., Amarneh, M., Al-Sa'ed, R., Zeeman, G., Gijzen, H. and Lettinga, G. (2003) 'Sewage characterisation as a tool for the application of anaerobic treatment in Palestine', *Environmental Pollution* 126: 115–22.

Marshall, G. (1996) 'Greywater re-use: hardware, health, environment and the law', *The Sixth International Permaculture Conference and Convergence*, Perth and Bridgetown, Western Australia.

Ogoshi, M., Suzuki, Y. and Asano, T. (2001) 'Water reuse in Japan', *Water Science and Technology* 43: 17–23.

Parkinson, J. and Tayler, K. (2003) 'Decentralized wastewater management in peri-urban areas in low-income countries', *Environment and Urbanization* 15: 75–90.

Plancenter (1997) 'Conceptual master plan for sewerage management at Ramallah District', Plancenter and Center for Engineering and Planning, Ramallah, Palestine.

Po, M., Nancarrow, B., Leviston, Z., Porter, N., Syme, G. and Kaercher, J. (2005) 'Predicting community behaviour in relation to wastewater reuse: what drives decisions to accept or reject?', Water for a Healthy Country National Research Flagship, CSIRO Land and Water, Australia's Commonwealth Scientific and Industrial Research Organization (CSIRO), Perth.

Prathapar, S., Jamrah, A., Al-Futaisi, A., Ahmad, M., Adawi, S., Al-Sidairi, S. and Al Harasi, A. (2005) 'Overcoming constraints in treated greywater reuse in Oman', *Desalination* 186: 177–86.

United Nations (UN) (2001) 'Chapter VI: Population, environment and development in urban settings', in *Population, Environment and Development: The Concise Report* (ST/ESA/SER.A/202), Population Division, Department of Economic and Social Affairs, UN, New York.

World Bank (2004) *West Bank and Gaza: Wastewater Treatment and Reuse Policy Note*, Water, Environment, Social and Rural Development Department, Middle East and North Africa Region.

About the authors

Dr Abu-Madi works with the Environmental and Water Studies Institute where he is involved in academic research and training activities, as well as community services. He holds a BSc in Chemical Engineering and Technology from the Institute of Technology, Banaras Hindu University in India; a diploma in Water Supply and Environmental Sanitation from Birzeit University in collaboration with IHE-Delft in the Netherlands; an MSc in Sanitary Engineering from IHE-Delft; and a PhD in Water and Environmental Engineering from the UNESCO-IHE Institute for Water Education and the Technical University of Delft. He has worked with many water and environmental organizations. Dr Abu-Madi is the research coordinator of PoWER (Global Partnership for Water

Education and Research), which has partnership with 18 leading institutions from all over the world.
Email: abumadi@birzeit.edu

Dr. Rashed Al-Sa'ed is an associate professor and a staff member at the Institute of Environmental and Water Studies, Birzeit University whose main research fields are wastewater treatment and appropriate sanitation.

Dr. Nidal Mahmoud is an associate professor and a staff member at the Institute of Environmental and Water Studies, Birzeit University, whose main research field is anaerobic digestion with emphasis on decentralized sanitation concepts.

Jamal Burnat is a water and environmental sanitation specialist in a food security programme at ACDI-VOCA.

CHAPTER 7

Can local people accept greywater technology?

Peter Laban

Important applied research into greywater (GW) use has been undertaken in the past five years with promising results, and demonstrating potential for replication and up-scaling. Project examples from Palestine and Jordan cited in this chapter and discussed elsewhere in this volume bear witness to that. However, many issues still need to be resolved. This chapter will challenge researchers and technicians with a number of questions that must be answered if research-tested technology has to find a place among local end-users in both rural and urban settings. Such questions relate to cultural acceptability, costs and benefits, required knowledge, and practicality. It is argued that in order to develop technology that can be used at scales where it can really impact sustainable water use, end-users or future clients need to be more involved in the problem analysis and design. Inspiration may be found for this in approaches developed in agricultural extension known as participatory technology development.

Introduction

The Aqaba Meeting (see the introduction to this volume) has taken stock of new insights and achievements in the search for low-cost and acceptable technologies to treat and use wastewater. This chapter will focus on the social and cultural acceptability of the use of GW in the Middle East. The research on these issues is urgent as many people in this region suffer from severe water scarcity and food insecurity. Technological contributions to solutions that respond to the demand for water at the household level are therefore a necessity. Such contributions will complement the search for more effective and participatory planning and policies in the water sector.

Important research has been undertaken especially in Palestine and Jordan to develop GW and wastewater treatment systems, both at the individual-household level or for clusters of households. As cited by Burnat and Eshtayah in this volume (Chapter 2), in Palestine, the GW contribution to daily household total wastewater production is about 80 per cent, while at least 60 per cent of GW can be recovered, treated, and used. This amount of wastewater, when properly treated, can be used for agriculture, resulting in saving fresh drinking water and reducing the frequency of emptying the cesspits. For instance in Palestine, septic tank upflow gravel filter plants have been constructed by the Palestinian Agriculture Relief Committees (PARC) for treatment of GW from a single house (300 of these units have been installed) or groups of up to 30 houses (7 of these communal units have been installed).

Some of these systems started working in January 1997, receiving GW flows of 500–20,000 litres/day. The treated effluents are mostly used by means of drip irrigation systems to irrigate home gardens. Where COD concentrations were generally very high (~1,270 mg/l) just after installation, the effluent quality improved gradually with time until a value of less than 200 mg COD/l was reached after 90 days. Technically, the treatment of grey wastewater in such plants and the use of effluent in unrestricted agriculture have a high potential for environmental protection and water conservation.

In Jordan for example – as shown by Suleiman and colleagues in this volume (Chapter 4) – two treatment technologies were used to treat GW in small rural communities in the north-eastern Badia. These included: 1) a septic tank followed by an intermittent sand filter (ISF); 2) an up-flow anaerobic sludge blanket (UASB). The septic tank–ISF approach demonstrated high treatment efficiency for physical, chemical and microbial contaminants. The sand filter system was effective in removing the pathogens indicated by *E. coli*. However, the performance of the UASB system in removing pathogens was improved after adding a zeolite filter. Although both systems were efficient in treating the typically strong GW, the UASB coupled with a zeolite filter was easier to operate and maintain, and was reckoned to be more cost effective.

In order for a certain technology to be adopted by local people, it needs to be embedded in their cultural and socioeconomic realities. This applies in both rural and urban settings. It is great to be able to demonstrate that a particular technology succeeds in treating wastewater – grey or black – in a way that is technically feasible and respects different ecological and quality/health criteria. However, if such a technology is financially unaffordable and does not consider the cultural and religious values of the host community, it will be very difficult to apply at scales that will lead to the desired impact. Moreover, people have not taken ownership of technologies introduced from outside and often do not see such technologies as parts of their daily lives.

There are four important questions that local people may raise when exposed to a new technology for treatment and use of GW. These are:

- Am I allowed to use it?
  How acceptable is this technology in view of my cultural and religious values?
- Can I afford it and/or does it reduce my living expenses?
  How affordable is this technology and what is the financial benefit to me?
- How difficult is it to use?
  What is the required knowledge to install, operate and maintain this technology?

- Does it give me more water that I can use in a safe way?
  How does it improve my access and rights to sufficient and good quality water?

This chapter reflects on these questions and attempts to reach answers that ensure that people will feel comfortable with such new technologies and will take ownership of its use and maintenance. Some approaches are available in other fields of research that have demonstrated how developing 'new' technology in a participatory way has a better chance of responding positively to the questions above. Some examples will be given at the end of this chapter.

Am I allowed to use it?

> Maybe what you, technician, say is valid, but how can we make use of it. In our culture it is even not allowed to put a bucket of water on the kitchen table if it is to be used for cleaning the floor of the house!

How acceptable is GW technology in view of cultural and religious values? In the Middle East there are strong taboos (which may or may not be based on Islamic scriptures) that make people hesitant to use water that has been used for other purposes and is no longer clean. As mentioned in the chapter by Dalahmeh and colleagues in this volume (Chapter 5), '[a]ccording to the teachings of Islam, water containing faeces or urine is considered unclean (*mutanajjis*). Because of this, some people are not content to discharge water from sinks and showers, and kitchen water (i.e. greywater) into the same cesspool as wastewater from toilets. In the case of kitchen GW, this may also stem from the fact that it contains some food remains, which are regarded as "God's gift"'. In the current technical jargon, water originating from normal household use (kitchen, shower and basins) is called GW, whereas when it comes from the toilets it is called blackwater. There seems to be some acceptance to the use of GW for irrigating vegetables and fruit trees. However this acceptance is still not without hesitation. Most probably this is also a matter of time. For instance, Jamrah and colleagues (2004) investigated the Omanis' perceptions towards the use of treated GW and found that about 82 per cent of the respondents were in favour of GW treatment and use in agricultural irrigation. In Palestine, Burnat and Eshtayah (Chapter 2) conclude that the acceptance of the local communities for the concept of treated wastewater use is not yet mature enough, although some people in poor rural areas have accepted GW treatment in their households. Local communities' awareness of the importance of this activity needs to be improved through relevant awareness campaigns and training.

The use of blackwater is often considered completely unclean. These taboos are strong and need to be faced in an open way. Experiments and water tests may help, but it will be a long process of awareness raising, education and dialogue that may need to begin in primary schools. In any case, the questions below also need to be answered in a satisfactory way, before taking this dialogue too far. It is interesting to note that in Singapore the use of bottled water that is produced from treated GW is now very widely accepted. In India, in the area around Bombay, farmers are hijacking trucks that transport black-water and waste, in order to use it to fertilize their crops, as soils get poorer and poorer and no longer produce sufficient food. Also in the Middle East there is increasing experience with possible ways to overcome these cultural constraints. In Palestine, technology has now been developed and is increasingly accepted where household wastewater is cleaned and used in glasshouses to irrigate vegetable crops like lettuce and tomatoes (personal reference: Monther Hind, 2008). Al-Jayyousi's chapter in this volume (Chapter 10) directly addresses the Islamic religion's approach to wastewater use. Al-Jayyousi argues that there need be no religious rejection of wastewater use, provided adequate safeguards are taken.

Can I afford it and/or does it reduce my living expenses?

> Well, this looks very impressive and I am sure it works at your research station, but if I have to buy it, it certainly will be too expensive. And when using it, I am not very convinced that my daily cost for water will be any less.

Good questions! As development workers, researchers, or technicians, we often cannot give a satisfactory response to these questions. It is essential that the technology be low-cost and easily installed in the poorer households if it is intended to be applied for a large number of beneficiaries. What is important is not only being able to buy the necessary equipment or materials and afford their cost, but also being able to get spare parts at the local market. Are they readily available? Can repairs be easily made at a low cost? Too often these aspects are ignored at the research and development stages. It is not certain that wastewater treatment-and-use technologies developed for larger institutions (offices, schools and university campuses) can be applied easily at smaller units (isolated houses in rural areas and individual units in apartment buildings).

The chapter by Abu-Madi and others in this volume (Chapter 6) outlines a study conducted in Palestine where the socioeconomic feasibility and public perceptions of GW systems and cesspits were compared. The study revealed that GW systems are superior to cesspits in terms of construction costs, operational costs, water consumption and saving in water consumption and water bills. However, the study also made clear that people are still not likely to pay the installation cost themselves. The main reasons behind public rejection to implement GW systems with their own funding were: 1) refusal to restructure the internal piping systems for separation of black and greywater; 2) refusal to use the treated effluent for garden irrigation; 3) unaffordable construction costs. This, especially in more urban environments, also may be related to a preference to be linked to central wastewater systems rather than making their own new investments. More work is still needed to clarify what the long-term financial benefits, which would offset the above-mentioned perceived barriers to invest in these systems by local people, are. In fact, Redwood – in his introduction to this volume – admits that the long-term financial feasibility of many types of GW systems is still not certain.

It is indeed important to break out of the conventional research and development (R&D) mind-set and focus on GW application in small units, in order to get the desired scale of impact. Further development of such technology, in cooperation with women and/or farmers who are its likely users, is essential to determine what are the bottlenecks and reasons behind the hesitation to use this technology and to explore how such technology can help people find solutions to the problems they face. The final section of this chapter shares some experiences with participatory technology development (PTD) approaches that have been successful in finding relevant solutions to perceived local problems.

How difficult is it to use?

Sir, maybe this is good for you in your own house. But I am not at all sure that I can handle this, that it does not take too much of my time, that it does not make my household or farm work more laborious.

In general, people are reluctant to introduce new things when they are not sure that it will help them, save time, and be easy to use. In many cases people will observe how others deal with the new thing, before they make their own decision about it. In Dutch this is known as 'looking the cat out of the tree'. This question and the one above are closely connected. A positive answer to only one question is not enough. Equipment and technology should be cheap and easy to use without much extra effort. In many cases, people may say that it is much easier to continue the practices they are accustomed to. Just proposing such ready-made technology, even if it is tested for those practical issues, often does not work.

Progress is being made in the right direction, however, as a research study in Palestine explains – see Burnat and Eshtayah in this volume (Chapter 2). In conjunction with the Qebia Womens' Cooperative, 48 pilot units of an on-site household GW treatment-and-use systems were installed in a village in Palestine. The research study assessed and audited the impact of these GW systems on environmental, health, and socioeconomic factors at the household level. The study concluded that the technology applied was low cost and that so long as experience and materials were locally available, there was no need for skilled personnel to operate and maintain the systems. Operational and maintenance costs as well as energy consumption costs were low (around US$20 per year) and the effluent was treated enough to be used. There is now a high demand for these systems in Qebia and surrounding villages. After the installation of the first 23 systems, another 25 systems were installed. However, this covers only 30 per cent of the demand.

It was found that the system could provide an amount of treated water for irrigation, which can produce more food. The water bill is reduced after using the treated GW, instead of freshwater, to irrigate the home garden. The expenditure on pumping out the cesspit is reduced dramatically at houses where GW used to be discharged to the cesspit. The beneficiaries feel and demonstrate ownership of the system, and take care of it so as to benefit from it.

Also, as illustrated in the last section of this chapter, people are more ready to accept solutions when they have been involved in developing them and when they have participated in the search for technical and maintenance solutions as well as in the final design of the technology.

Does it give me more water that I can use in a safe way?

Yes, it looks interesting. But if I install this thing, will it save me water? Is it really true that the water is safe and that my children won't get sick?

People will be reluctant to use GW when they do not see the immediate benefits of acquiring cheaper, or higher quantities of, water with less effort. In fact, the extra benefits of a particular innovation often must be much more significant than the difference in (extra) cost when compared with their previous setup. In pragmatic 'back-of-the-envelope' economic analyses, this is very convincingly expressed as ($\Delta Y/\Delta X > 2$). In other words, the extra (or marginal) benefits should be two times more than the extra (marginal) cost. This is a general rule of thumb, reflecting the risks (cost and other risks) that people implicitly calculate before making decisions. And they are often right – how often has it happened that the nice new equipment did not function properly, did not deliver what was promised, or had to be simply put in the bin. Scaling-up and distributing equipment through the market almost always will require involving private enterprise. But often, private enterprise, when it sees a gap in the market, will 'sell' such new equipment very convincingly without sufficient quality control. Government services therefore have a regulatory role and responsibility. Involving customers in the design of the technology is often very useful.

Participatory technology development

One of the most critical factors in the success of such interventions in communities is the degree of local public involvement in the decision making. It is suggested that involving end-users or clients in the analysis of difficulties they face and in the design of a new technology will pay off. Of course, this does not mean that the whole population of a country or an area has to participate. A representative selection of households will often suffice. If the technology is successful – and responds positively to the four questions above, it will spread by itself and in a short time commerce will take over for further distribution.

Harris (2000) noted that the involvement of, and communication with, the communities in projects and policy development can be achieved in a variety of different ways, such as information giving, information gathering, traditional consultation, bounded dialogue and open dialogue. Also, it is argued that community involvement relies much on participatory rural (or rapid) appraisal (PRA) tools (Pretty and Vodouhê, 1998). PRA is an efficient and cost-effective way of gathering information from local people. PRA techniques rely on identifying an overall picture, rather than looking for statistical significance, and they also emphasize the importance of local knowledge. Providing the public with an effective means of participation and building trust with the communities by involving them in the planning process early on – collecting data, assessing needs, building capacity, selecting alternative sites and technologies, and having an input into the management wheel – is a most important tool that ensures the cooperative management of community resources and enhances project quality and sustainability (Ockelford and Reed, 2002).

Involving local people in the planning process is an important step. Another step is involving them in the technology development process. A lot of thinking has been done already in agriculture on how to better involve farmers (both men and women) in the innovation of their farming practices. This has become known as participatory technology development (PTD) (Van Veldhuizen et al., 1997). PTD is a participatory research and development approach developed on the premise that effective local technological innovation requires bringing together on an equal basis the local knowledge and experiences of end-users/clients (farmers and women in households) with those from research and extension agencies. PTD, developed at the end of the 1980s by a wide group of NGOs and other development practitioners, is a systematically-facilitated and community-led process, a series of activities, in which local constraints (e.g. to agricultural development, water management or use of domestic water) are identified and analysed. Subsequently, together with support agencies and research, potentially appropriate technical innovations are selected with these end-users, after which they go through a process of piloting, studying, experimenting, monitoring and evaluation of these innovations to arrive at well founded solutions/technologies that can be used for further dissemination. PTD forms a part of the conceptual and methodological thinking that has developed since the late 1980s on how to better respect farmers' knowledge and come to more sustainable agriculture while reducing external inputs. This development approach has become known among agricultural practitioners as low-external input and sustainable agriculture (LEISA). Where LEISA emphasizes the need to find synergy and complementarity in different agricultural technologies and practices, it leans heavily on PTD to develop such technologies and practices with farmers and researchers in a participatory way. It is evident that in such PTD processes, ample consideration is given to the four questions mentioned above. A part of the technology development process has to take into account these concerns. They will surface logically as long as the future clients are involved from the start. Six different steps can be recognized in the PTD process:

1. getting started in specific communities;
2. understanding problems and opportunities – priority setting;
3. looking for potential solutions to try out;
4. experimenting (participatory farmer research);
5. sharing the results = end-user based extension;
6. sustaining the innovation process (people taking research initiatives themselves).

A trainer's guide for PTD facilitators was tested and subsequently published, in association with ETC Netherlands BV, Leusden (Van Veldhuizen et al., 1997). It was translated into other languages, including Arabic, Bahasa Indonesian, Chinese, French and Portuguese. The Arabic translation of this guide was carried out by the Coptic Evangelical Organization for Social Services (CEOSS), a 55-year old NGO in Egypt with a broad spectrum of community-based activities in more than 150 rural villages and towns. The following case study was one of CEOSS's first PTD activities, which started in 1996. This formed the basis for a now strongly developed PTD farmer network, which produces ecological products for the urban market.

Developing participatory technology development in rural Egypt

One example where PTD was successfully used to introduce an adapted technology to solve major problems is the 1990s pilot project in Sharoona and Nassareya in Middle Egypt near Minya, where a problem existed with solid household waste in densely populated villages and small rural towns in the Nile Valley.

As a part of an important change process towards enhancing the self-reliance of its target communities, CEOSS used a PTD approach to create synergy between solving garbage problems in the home and finding ways to replace chemical fertilisers in the farm. The participatory process involved women in analysing their current problems and led to the testing of an innovation to achieve greater cleanliness and hygiene in the livestock stables and family living areas. By concentrating organic household waste, manure, and urine in a pit in the in-house stable, an organic fertiliser was produced that had much higher nitrogen content than the traditional manure. At the same time, the garbage recycling through improved stables resulted in considerable time savings for the women, and improved health conditions for the families and income-earning opportunities for the women. The project strategy was built heavily on a gender-sensitive PTD approach and focused on garbage recycling by the women and improved use of fertilisers by the men.

PRA exercises were held in two representative rural towns and demonstrated clearly that disposal of household wastewater and garbage were the most important problem for women. Male farmers gave high importance to reducing the cost of chemical fertilisers. Discussions in the communities then guided a project proposal to develop a PTD approach. Implementation started in January 1997 with a PTD training and design workshop with one of the three farmer groups selected by the communities. Cleaner and healthier conditions in houses and streets were a top priority for women. After a participatory process in a series of workshops, discussions, and visits, it was decided to try out an innovation that consisted of making a pit in the in-house stables where manure, straw, and urine from the stable and other organic waste, as well as kitchen ash from the house, were collected over a two- to three-day period. The improved manure was then dug out and transported to the field as organic fertiliser.

Having fields with similar soil conditions the farmers, who were particularly interested in reducing the cost of chemical fertilisers, decided to start small experiments in subgroups of about four to six persons. The experiments would compare yield, plant development and effects on soils of three different treatments: reduced quantities of chemical fertiliser, use of bio-fertiliser, and use of cow manure. After only nine months, about 30 farmers working together in farmer experimenting groups acquired a taste for more systematic experimentation with different crop practices and claimed that they would continue this with or without support from CEOSS. Other farmers showed interest in joining the experimenting groups or started experiments on their own. The initial results of the fertiliser experiments indicated that it would be possible to maintain yields of wheat and other crops and reduce cost despite decreased applications of chemical fertilisers.

The innovation of the compost pit in the stable inside the house proved to be highly successful. It considerably reduced the time women spent each day bringing soil from the fields to dry the stable and carrying household waste to the garbage dumps near the riverside. At the same time, it became easier to clean the stables and unnecessary to clean the animals every day at the river or the irrigation canals. Moreover, the cleaner stables and animals made it possible to obtain much cleaner milk and to improve the health conditions of both animals and humans. Also men benefited from this innovation, as they no longer had to carry manure every day to their fields. Men believed they obtained much richer manure than before (although this still has to be proved). Initially, 60 women were participating in six groups. This number has rapidly increased to about 100 women in the second year, and more than 50 additional women have asked if they also can try out this innovation.

Such a PTD approach geared to addressing the water supply problems of low-income, water stressed communities may yield interesting results regarding the development and implementation of relevant GW technology and associated practices.

Conclusion

Integrated management of water and wastewater in small communities in the Middle East and North Africa (MENA) is essential in order to address serious concerns over water scarcity and pollution, meet the demand for convenience, and protect public health (Bakir, 2001). Sustainable and integrated management of GW in rural communities includes production of clean GW beneficial for irrigation without negative impacts on health and environment. This management is directly affected by the awareness of local people and depends on the regular follow-up and maintenance of the treatment facilities by house owners and housewives. The driving forces behind use of GW, its separation from blackwater, and its treatment include religious attitudes and beliefs, scale of economy, and the need to maximize the use of the available water (Dalahmeh et al., Chapter 5 this volume). Participatory approaches to the development of appropriate technologies are critical to success and to providing convincing answers to the four questions raised in this chapter. PTD could be a useful way to make that happen.

References

Bakir, H.A. (2001) 'Sustainable wastewater management for small communities in the Middle East and North Africa', *Journal of Environmental Management* 61: 319–28.

Harris, R. (2000) 'Why is dialogue different?', *Elements* 2, Environment Council, UK.

Jamrah, A., Al-Futaisi, A., Prathapar, S., Ahmad, M. and Al Harasi, A. (2004) 'Evaluating greywater reuse potential for sustainable water resources management in the Sultanate of Oman', *The International Conference on Water Demand Management*, Dead Sea, Jordan.

Ockelford, J. and Reed, B. (2002) *Participatory Planning for Integrated Rural Water Supply and Sanitation Programmes: Guidelines and Manual*, Water, Engineering and Development Centre, Loughborough University, England.

Pretty, J. and Vodouhê, S.D. (1998) 'Using rapid or participatory rural appraisal', in B.E. Swanson, R.P. Bentz and A.J. Sofranko (eds), *Improving Agricultural Extension: A Reference Manual*, Food and Agriculture Organisation of the United Nations, Rome.

Van Veldhuizen, L., Waters-Bayer, A. and De Zeeuw, H. (1997) *Developing Technology with Farmers: A Trainer's Guide for Participatory Learning*, ZED Books, London.

About the author

At the time he contributed to this book, Peter Laban was the Regional Coordinator of the Euro-Med Participatory Water Resources Scenarios (EMPOWERS) Programme, a partnership programme funded by the European Commission in Jordan, Palestine, and Egypt and implemented by CARE International

(2003–2007). He has since joined IUCN's Regional Office for West Asia as its regional programme coordinator. He also supervises IUCN's Regional Water Resources and Dry-land (REWARD) Programme. REWARD and EMPOWERS are/were facilitating a stakeholder dialogue approach for improved participatory planning in water resource management and development activities at the community, watershed, and governorate levels. Laban has extensive international experience, which he gained from working in South Asia, West Africa, and the Middle East. He worked on natural resource management, community forestry, local water governance, and community development and was involved in many implementation projects and research and evaluation studies.

Email: peter.laban@iucn.org

CHAPTER 8

Lessons from a participatory approach to household greywater use in Jordan

Noel Keough, Samira Smirat and Stan Benjamin

Water management literature points to the persistent lack of effective citizen and community engagement in water management throughout the world. In this chapter we report on the efforts to engage five Jordanian communities in a participatory research process to implement, evaluate and modify a decentralized greywater (GW) technology. We discuss key issues relating to the implementation of the project, including project management and decision-making, planning for effective operation and maintenance, challenges for the long-term sustainability and scale-up of decentralized GW systems, potential benefits and risks to public health, and economic feasibility.

We pose several challenges to, and recommendations for, more effective decentralized GW use strategies. Project management protocols should be agreed upon by all parties. Water management projects can and should be a catalyst for women's empowerment. Ethical issues of health and environmental impacts need careful consideration. Privatization of water and waste infrastructure presents important equity issues that require careful attention. To date, debate has focused on the technical and economic advantages of decentralized water technologies. Reflection on our work in Karak highlights the equally important cultural, social, and political dimensions of the debate. This chapter proposes a new role for the professional or expert in a more decentralized and integrated approach to water management – one that is much more profoundly integrated and collaborative than the conventional model. Partnership is a key. Roles are less rigid and more flexible as all partners define their contribution and working relationships.

Introduction

Between 2003 and 2006, PLAN:NET Ltd. (P:N), a Canadian development consulting company with Middle East regional offices in Amman, Jordan, was involved in Greywater Treatment and Use for Poverty Reduction in Jordan (Phase II), an applied research project designed to test the feasibility of the scale-up of household GW treatment-and-use systems in five peri-urban communities in the Karak Governorate in southern Jordan. The Karak greywater project was funded by the International Development Research Centre (IDRC), Canada.

The executing agency for this project was the Inter-Islamic Network on Water Resources Development and Management (INWRDAM). P:N was invited to play an enabling role as a facilitator of a community participation process to ensure successful community involvement in the installation and operation of the GW technologies. This project is discussed in the chapter by Bino and others in this volume (Chapter 3).

This chapter begins with a summary of the water management in Jordan and its international context, with particular attention to the growing consensus of the need for deeper community involvement in the design and implementation of water and sanitation systems. The summary is followed by a review and analysis of the GW project. We first describe the project's communities and the technologies employed. We then present the participation and sustainable development model informing the execution of the community participation component (CPC) of the project. Next, we present the activities associated with the project, the major issues encountered and the community outcomes achieved. Finally, we discuss lessons learned that we believe are of value to future water management projects in Jordan, MENA countries and beyond. Of particular importance, in our view, is the relationship between the technical and cultural dimensions of local water management.

The international context of water management in Jordan

The Jordan GW project was set within a critical regional water-management challenge. It is common knowledge that the Middle East faces very challenging water-management issues. Beaumont (2002) argues that among the countries of the Middle East the challenges range from minor to severe. His analysis makes the claim that Jordan is in fact in the worst water deficit-and-supply situation of any MENA country. He points out that aquifers are already being mined to meet supply and that merely diverting water from irrigation to residential and industrial uses will not meet demand to 2025. He also argues that alternative supply through desalination will be a costly endeavour and through diversion from Lebanon via Israel will be politically unrealistic.

At less than 125 m³/capita/year, water supply in Jordan is already well below the widely accepted water scarcity mark of 1,000 m³/capita/year, and is being used at 148.5 per cent of the sustainable supply (Alkhaddar et al., 2005). Rafid Alkhaddar and others (2005) report that by 2010, Jordan will face the prospect of seven million inhabitants consuming a mere 85 m³/capita/year. More than 60 per cent of the population of Jordan is not yet served by sewerage services. Exacerbating the meagre water supply is the level of poverty in Jordan. Alkhaddar et al. (2005) reported that in 2002, 7 per cent of Jordanians lived on less than US$2/day and 11.7 per cent of Jordanians lived below the national absolute poverty line.

An important dimension of the water management landscape in Jordan is the recent push toward privatization. In 1997, Jordan embarked on a privatization policy that included provision of water services. The water management privatization programme began in Amman and is being progressively implemented in other parts of the country (Abu-Shams and Rabadi, 2003). Pricing is another key aspect of the water management context. Asit Biswas (2005) argues that water pricing is a complex, contentious and necessary issue. In recent times Jordan has accepted the concept of water pricing. Its policy calls for cost recovery of water management infrastructure along with a pricing regime to facilitate cost recovery (Abu-Shams and Rabadi, 2003).

Asit Biswas (2001) has documented the emergence of international water management frameworks and debates over the past 20 years. He argues that water issues are too complex to be the domain of a single government ministry or of water professionals alone. Solutions to water problems encompass water availability, management regimes and capacities, technological and economic capacities, social and environmental conditions, education levels, and the political climate. He writes that 'one can argue that the time has already come when all major water issues should be analysed, reviewed and resolved within an overall societal and development context, otherwise the main objectives of water management such as poverty alleviation, equitable development and environmental conservation cannot be achieved' (ibid: 490). This viewpoint is consistent with the declarations from the Mexico (World Water Congress, 2006) and Japan World Water Congresses (World Water Congress, 2005) and with key water management strategies identified from both the 2002 World Summit on Sustainable Development and the Millennium Development Goals (United Nations, 2007). Biswas (2001) observes that contrary to what is considered by the above-mentioned sources as best practice, water management policy is still too uni-sectoral, too engineering oriented and too hierarchical and top-down.

The importance of decentralized peri-urban wastewater recovery

Given the very limited water resources in the MENA countries and in particular in Jordan, there is a strong consensus that wastewater recovery is a critical component of water management in the region. Meanwhile, there is a growing critique of centralized sewerage systems as a silver bullet solution to wastewater treatment and recovery. A World Bank review estimated the capital costs of such systems in capital cities of eight developing countries, where the per capita income ranged between US$600–4,000 (based on 1980 prices), at a total household annual amortized capital and operation and maintenance cost of US$150–650 (Mara, 1998). In smaller cities and low-density urban and peri-urban areas, the costs are even more prohibitive, since for various reasons economies of scale are not as great as in large dense cities. The Karak GW project is an example of the most decentralized solution – the household level. IDRC points to the fact that even today urban agriculture (UA), operating at a household, neighbourhood, or community-cluster scale, is providing a significant portion of Jordan's production at a cost of only 20 per cent of the water used in more extensive farming practices (Faruqui et al.,

2001). The design, installation, and management of efficient, reliable, safe, and effective decentralized GW use systems is an important contribution to the multi-faceted needs of water management in developing countries.

The human dimension of these systems is the focus of this chapter. The centrality of the human dimension of water management is highlighted by the Dublin Principles (ibid), which affirm that water is a social and economic good, that water management should be participatory and integrated and that women should play a central role in water management.

In light of the potential for decentralized wastewater recovery, a 1998 conference convened by IDRC, IWMC, and INWRDAM recommended 'assess[ing] how to move beyond simply involving communities and water users' associations in decision-making and empowering them' and 'develop[ing] gender analysis of community-based water management projects in Muslim countries to more effectively bring women into community-based water management' (ibid: 26). The findings of the conference support the contention that culturally driven behaviour change will be required to create sustainable water management and that inter-sectoral and inter-governmental cooperation will be crucial to the task. In an overview of the principles of water management in Islam, Naser Faruqui and colleagues (Faruqui et al, 2001) highlight the consensus among conference participants that an Islamic perspective on community-based water management would require mandatory community input, consultation with all members of the community, proactive individuals contributing to the solution not just demanding things, and grassroots change with community members working together and educating each other.

It is important to note that these principles are not exclusive to Islam or for that matter to developing countries. The Rocky Mountain Institute (2004) in Colorado, USA, recently completed a study of eight US communities. Through interviews with water-management officials and stakeholders, the recommendations for wastewater project implementation included working closely with regulatory officials, planning for genuine substantial public participation in the planning process, attending carefully to the values of the community and carefully and clearly defining and measuring the problem.

Methodology

Principles of citizen participation

Now let us turn to a discussion of the philosophical, theoretical, and practical underpinnings of the participatory model employed in Al-Amer. Brazilian adult educator Paulo Freire provides the philosophical and theoretical underpinnings of a family of approaches that can be grouped under the heading of participatory action research. Freire (1968) argues that development has to be about the empowerment of individuals to understand their world and to act to change it for the better. He cautions professionals that even with the best of intentions, the act of extension in whatever sector it takes place, means that those carrying it out need to go to 'another part of the world' to 'normalize it' according to their way of viewing reality. In contrast, first and foremost a Freirian approach would counsel professionals to begin with an understanding of the world they are entering rather than seek to make it mirror their own world.

Robert Chambers is perhaps the most well-known practitioner of participatory action research approaches and popularizer of a particular approach known as participatory rural (or rapid) appraisal (PRA). Chambers' approaches are widely known and practiced across the MENA region. Chambers echoes Freire when he writes that 'the essence of PRA is changes and reversals – of role, behaviour, relationship and learning' (Chambers, 1997: 75). For Chambers, PRA is an approach and methodology for learning about rural life and conditions from, with and by rural people. It is a family of approaches and methods to enable rural people to share, enhance and analyse their knowledge of life and conditions, and to plan and act to improve their lives. Moreover, it is a philosophy and way of life that stresses self-critical awareness and commitment to the poor, weak, and vulnerable.

The three foundations of PRA are: 1) the behaviour and attitudes of outsiders, who facilitate, not dominate; 2) the shift of methods from closed to open, from individual to group, from verbal to visual, and from measuring to comparing; 3) partnership and sharing of information, experience, food and training between insiders and outsiders and between organizations. Chambers argues that the traditional research process does not work because in practice quantitative and statistical error and measurement constraints limit its effectiveness, that professional biases distort the research process, that an inappropriate transference of the professionals' reality imposes itself on the community, and that the unequal power relations between the conventional researcher and the community distort the research process and outcomes. In sum, Chambers proposes PRA as a means to provide the capabilities for individuals to take control of their own well-being and livelihoods, and to ensure that change will be sustainable.

P:N has been practicing participatory community-development for over 20 years. The following principles approximate P:N's approach to community participation in general, and to its approach to the GW project in particular:

- Approach each situation with humility and respect.
- Understand the potential for local knowledge.
- Adhere to democratic practice.
- Acknowledge diverse ways of knowing.
- Maintain a sustainability vision.
- Put reality before theory.
- Embrace uncertainty.
- Recognize the relativity of time and efficiency.
- Take a holistic approach.
- Exercise an option for community – people first.

Results

The community

The Al-Amer villages that make up the project site for the greywater project belong to Al-Kasser District of the Karak Governorate. The villages encompass an area of about 17 km². The total population of the five villages (Al-Jada'a, Mugayer, Ariha, Masa'ar, and Abu-Trabah) is approximately 7,856 people. According to statistics from the Ministry of Social Development, 24 per cent of people work in government positions, 20 per cent work in the army, 23 per cent are retired, 16 per cent work in agriculture, 7 per cent work in the private sector, and 5 per cent are unemployed. According to the World Bank (2008) indicators, the unemployment rate of women in Jordan is almost double that of men.

Due to the water crisis, many of the region's farmers have abandoned their lands to take low-profile, but regular salaried jobs in the army. In many cases, women and sons, or hired farm workers, have replaced husbands and fathers in farm work. There is no central sewer system in the project area – all households use septic tanks. Since there are no artesian wells or water springs in the area, Al-Amer is serviced by the water authority. Water is delivered to homes via a network on average twice a week. The supply is unreliable, so most people resort to the purchase of water from tankers at a very high price, approximately JOD6/m³ (based on exchange rates of May 2009, JOD1 = US$1.41). Most of the farmers depend on rainwater for irrigation, at times supplemented with tap water.

The technology

The goal of the GW treatment project is 'to help the peri-urban poor in Jordan preserve precious freshwater, achieve food security, and generate income, while helping to protect the environment'. Phase I of the project involved the design, construction and installation of GW treatment-and-use systems in a small number of households in Ein Al-Baida, Tafila, Jordan. The goal of phase II is to demonstrate the feasibility of the GW treatment technology at a much larger scale (300 households) and to determine the feasibility for nation-wide implementation of the GW systems. Based on the evaluation of phase I, a cluster of five peri-urban communities in the Karak Governorate were invited to participate in phase II.

It was decided that in phase II, both systems tested in phase I would again be installed – the four-barrel system and the confined trench system (CT) (see Chapter 3 in this volume for a more detailed technical description of the systems).

Evaluation of phase I

The P:N team was charged with conducting the evaluation of phase I of the GW project, organizing the five communities invited to participate in phase II and establishing the monitoring and evaluation framework for phase II.

The evaluation of phase I showed that from a technical standpoint the project was well executed. In fact, support was received from other donors (the EU and the Jordanian Ministry of Planning) for the installation of more systems throughout the country. The evaluation found definite economic and social benefits to the systems premised on the systems being free, but cautioned that the cost–benefit of the systems had to be revisited based on an owner pay scenario. Also the evaluation found that the CT systems delivered better water quality than the two- or four-barrel systems and that overall only 56 per cent of the systems met Jordanian standards for restricted irrigation. It also noted the prevalence of odour and soil salinity problems. On the social and capacity-building side of the project, among the issues raised in the evaluation were the need to strengthen training on system operation and maintenance and on agricultural methods, to broaden training opportunities to include topics like water conservation and environmental education, to establish a more transparent household selection process, to intensify efforts to incorporate gender issues into the project, and to mobilize a community engagement process prior to beneficiary selection and system installation. Limited success in targeting poor households for system installation also was noted in the evaluation report (PLAN:NET, 2004).

The process of citizen participation – phase II

The GW project's community participation strategy was developed to fulfil the objectives of the project and to establish the means for the community to continue to address community development needs independently, beyond the scope and lifespan of the project. During the mobilization phase, the project partners established criteria for project site selection and agreed upon a project site. This was followed by research to determine the key stakeholders in the selected community.

Meetings were held with local leaders, partners, the municipality, local NGOs, and relevant local government officials, and aimed at generating support for and acceptance of the project among the community. A large part of the community was made aware of, and expressed support for, the project. P:N established a liaison with a local NGO and an agreement was signed between P:N and the NGO to ensure the involvement of the community in all activities of the project. A local stakeholder committee (LSC) composed of community members from each of the project communities, including system users as well as project-team members, was formed to build and enhance community involvement in the project. The LSC played a crucial role in representing community interests and building support for the project. P:N and the LSC worked closely with INWRDAM on the selection of beneficiaries by developing a list of potential beneficiaries for the five villages and conducting field visits to make the final selection of beneficiaries based on technical and socioeconomic criteria – criteria that were modified during the field visits.

In May 2005, PRA training was conducted in the community. The training incorporated a baseline survey of the community and a community needs assessment. As a result of the community needs assessment, a proposal-writing workshop was held, leading to the drafting of a proposal to the Global Environmental Facility (GEF) for funding that would support the activities of the greywater project. In January 2006, word was received that the proposal was successful and an agreement was formally signed between the community and GEF.

The P:N team was charged with developing a monitoring and evaluation framework for the project. Following the completion of the framework, an initial monitoring survey was carried out in January 2006. The survey provided the first rigorous assessment of the project progress. The objectives of the survey were to monitor the progress of the technical, social, economic and agriculture components of the project, to record the extent to which objectives of phase II of the project were being achieved, and to measure the impact of the project on the beneficiaries and the community. The data was collected from beneficiaries through a formal survey. The survey team consisted of P:N personnel, LSC members, and a representative of the project partner – the Royal Society for the Conservation of Nature (RSCN). The survey was conducted simultaneously in the five villages. The process took three working days to complete.

Household survey findings

In total, 52 out of 103 beneficiary households who had up to that time received a GW system were surveyed, making up approximately 50 per cent of all GW systems in use in the five villages. The monitoring survey was carried out using a three-stage PRA approach: preparation and mobilization, data collection, and data analysis and reporting. The most significant findings of the survey include the following:

- The vast majority of households had not previously used GW. About 10 per cent had systems installed in phase I of the project. The average period the system had been used was 8.75 months, including those systems installed in phase I. Thirteen households (25 per cent) had been using the system for over a year. Thirty-four households (65 per cent) had been using the system for less than six months. The families surveyed were all low-income families. The average family size was eight people. The average land holding was 1,728 m² (approximately 1.25 dunums). The majority of beneficiaries used the CT system and expressed satisfaction with the system.

- In order of frequency of response, beneficiaries joined the system to conserve water and save on water bills (77 per cent), because irrigation would be easier (29 per cent), to save on time and effort in general (27 per cent), to save on pumping out the septic tank (25 per cent), and to ensure greater water availability (2 per cent). Overall the beneficiaries rated the system as good (42 per cent), very good (40 per cent) and excellent (12 per cent). Only one respondent claimed the system was weak.
- The average monthly savings in the household water bill was JOD1.76. This was calculated by comparing the pre- and post-system water bills for each household. Some families experienced higher bills, likely due to an expansion of garden plots in response to greater water availability.
- All the beneficiaries contributed to the installation of the system by preparing the land, either themselves or by hiring labour. On average, beneficiaries invested JOD17 to install and maintain the systems. Savings from water bills, septic tank pumping, and electricity bills averaged JOD15 per household. Sixty-three per cent of the savings realized through the systems were used to purchase food.
- With an alternative source for water, most of the beneficiaries were expecting an improvement in production from fruit trees. Three households reported a greater total and diversity in production – most likely those households who had the system for over a year. Fifty per cent of households reported an increase in the production from trees. One household developed a whole new garden following the installation of the system.
- The GW systems were generally functioning well. Beneficiaries' greatest concerns were odours and environmental problems (mosquitoes and flies). Odour, flies and mosquitoes were identified as problems by 61 per cent, 25 per cent, and 14 per cent of the beneficiary households respectively. Beneficiaries reported some maintenance problems. There were some complaints of calcification and blockage of the irrigation lines and of faulty pumps. As a result of the problems encountered, a number of beneficiaries have at times disconnected the pump from the electricity supply.
- Ninety per cent of the households with systems installed reported that neighbours had asked about the systems, and the majority of beneficiaries recommended the systems to neighbours. Forty neighbours were also included in the survey. The majority of neighbours surveyed reported they would like to obtain a system.
- The community played an important role in promoting the project and in the beneficiary selection process. The LSC members took their role and responsibilities seriously and were a link to the wider community and to the direct beneficiaries. The majority of people report having first heard about the systems from an LSC member.
- Women of the households were mainly the ones in charge of cleaning the system. However, men played a significant role. Fifty-four per cent

of the systems were cleaned solely by women. Thirty-three per cent of the systems were cleaned solely by men. In two per cent of the systems, husbands and wives played a joint role in cleaning, and in eight per cent of households wives and children cleaned the systems. The average cleaning time was approximately one hour.

- Most of the beneficiaries stated that men and women benefited differently from the project. Men benefited economically. Women realized a saving of time, effort, and workload, which left them with more time to take care of their families and other productive matters. Responses from some women indicated an ambiguity about the benefit of the system. It seems that some women were experiencing greater work loads when they took on the responsibility for the system.

- Forty-six per cent of the respondents claimed they had not increased their knowledge through the management of the system, while 38 per cent claimed they had. Increased knowledge was reported with respect to system operation and benefits, system maintenance and cleaning, community issues, and the importance of water. Similarly, 52 per cent of the respondents claimed they had not increased their skills, while 33 per cent had done so in the areas of maintenance and cleaning, system usage, irrigation, and community involvement.

Analysis of findings

Several issues emerged from the analysis of the survey results and from P:N team's reflection on project management, methodology and process of community engagement. These included project management and decision-making, system operation and maintenance, project sustainability, public health concerns, economic feasibility, and success of technology transfer and scale-up.

One of the most contentious issues was the management and decision-making process. Communication among project team members and between project team members and the LSC was problematic. Although in principle a 'participatory' approach was an explicit expectation of the project, the project team members and the LSC were unable to establish a mutually agreeable management and decision-making protocol. Among the project team and LSC members, the definition of participation varied from providing in-kind labour for system installation to practicing equal power in all project management decisions – hiring, project scheduling, system monitoring and evaluation.

Despite the recommendations of the evaluation of phase I, the monitoring survey suggested that operation and maintenance training was not sufficient. As a result, operation and maintenance issues similar to those encountered in phase I arose in phase II. It was unclear to what extent those issues were inherent in the system design and to what extent they were a matter of insufficient training.

The issues raised in the survey responses with respect to system training and maintenance highlight a key issue for the project. How will project partners ensure that, in addition to providing sufficient training, once the project is complete the community will develop the capacity to maintain and repair the systems on a sustainable basis? This question can only be answered in the long term.

The operation and maintenance issues identified through the monitoring survey highlighted the potential for negative health effects as a result of poor system performance. Potential negative effects included the inappropriate use of GW (e.g. on vegetable crops), the use of water that did not meet water quality standards for indirect irrigation, and the spread of diseases associated with flies and mosquitoes.

It is too early to quantify with any precision the economic costs and benefits associated with the systems. The biggest question mark remains whether there is a reasonable economic benefit after the full cost of purchasing the system is taken into account. A related issue is whether in a national policy climate of cost recovery and privatization, there is the potential for ongoing government subsidization of these systems.

Half of the 300 planned GW systems had been installed as of March 2006. Most people were quite satisfied with the systems, but there were emerging and mounting problems with maintenance and operation. The total number of systems installed was less than anticipated. However, this may be a positive aspect of the project and reflect the real absorption capacity of the community. It may be counterproductive to push too hard to meet an arbitrary system installation target.

Conclusion

Problem definition should precede prescription of a solution

While there is little doubt that water management is a pressing issue in Jordan, there was resistance in the communities to the imposition of a solution to a problem that had been defined independently of the community's input. Two assumptions were made prior to the engagement with the communities: 1) that water management is the primary issue in the community; 2) that a particular technology is the most appropriate response to the water management issue. This begs the question: at what stage in a process should the community be engaged?

In addition, it was clear that the community confronted a host of issues simultaneously, including employment, local economic development, housing, health care, education, energy supply, gender roles and equity. Water management interventions are vital, but singular intervention in communities that generally struggle with many issues is not a sustainable approach. Water management interventions should be planned and implemented within an integrated approach to community sustainability and communities should be partners in the processes of issue prioritization and technology selection.

Project management protocols should be agreed upon by all parties

The issue of project management arose early on in the project. In the conventional approach, professionals manage; moreover, technical professionals manage. In participatory approaches there is a much greater demand for co-management or community-led management with all professionals playing a supportive, facilitative or consultative role. The participatory process used to engage the community kindled community aspirations to be masters of their own houses. As a result, a struggle ensued between project team members and the community as to how the project should be managed.

Project ownership has to be explicitly and transparently resolved

The assumption of the project was that community members would operate and maintain the GW systems on their own – that they would be the owners. At what point does this ownership begin? Are the systems the property of the project lead agency? At what point in time do they become the property of the beneficiaries?

Water management projects can, and should be a catalyst for women's empowerment

The project demonstrates not only that women can be included as full participants in projects, but that the inclusion of women can provide a powerful 'value added' to the project. Women play a vital role in the success of both projects. In Karak, the monitoring survey demonstrated the key role women play in the successful operation and maintenance of the systems and in the generation of economic benefits via enhanced household garden production. Women initially played a peripheral role, but with a clear mandate to enhance equal gender participation in the projects, the project team was able to facilitate the emergence of women as key players in the project.

With women playing such a prominent role in the success of these systems, it would be wise to consider GW system implementation within a wider gender and development context. Methodologies – such as the Canadian International Development Agency (CIDA) Gender and Development Policy – exist that could be used to design such a program. Three pillars of the CIDA approach are that women not only participate through their labour, but that they have an equal role in decision-making, and that projects advance the full realization of human rights of women and girls and promote the equal access to and control over the resources and benefits of development (CIDA, 1999).

Technical solutions should respond to socio-culturally defined problems

Is water management a technical or a socio-cultural issue? Obviously, it is both. However, the P:N team found itself in a contractual partnership with an engineering organization that appeared to make the assumption that the role of the community participation partner (P:N) was public relations, or gaining community acceptance of the planned implementation of the GW technology. This raises the following question. Is water management a matter of social engineering to ensure the smooth operation of a given technological solution, or is the search for an appropriate technological response to a problem embedded in a larger social-cultural process? In other words, is it the technology or the community that drives the project? In our view, it has to be the community. And this has profound implications for the planning and management of water management projects. Community engagement has to come much earlier, be much more profound, and be afforded significantly more resources in order for water management interventions to be effective and sustainable.

More rigorous scale-up strategies are required to ensure success

There is a world of difference between a controlled experiment in a few households, or even a few communities, and implementation of a proven technology at a national scale. Among the questions the scale-up attempted in this project brings to the fore are the following: Is there a reliable supply of materials for the construction and maintenance of these systems? Will training efforts be directed to building capacity of each household to maintain and operate the system independently, or to building local technical capacity of technicians to service the systems through the market? Will the state or local governments establish and maintain the capacity to maintain the systems as a core government service? Each strategy requires very different training investments, very different policy regimes, and very different greywater system design considerations.

Ethical issues of health and environment impacts need more attention

More work needs to be done to understand the ethical issues associated with the promotion of decentralized water management. How is the level of risk of system malfunction, which may endanger health or the environment, established and distributed? What management or monitoring systems are required to minimize such dangers? What are the relative responsibilities of the state, system providers, system owners, and indeed the donors to maintain well-functioning and safe GW use systems?

Implications of privatization of water and waste infrastructure are not sufficiently addressed

This project grappled with the issue of access to water management services in a climate of privatization. There was concern in both cases that the poorest members of the community not be excluded from access to services. At least in the demonstration phase, the poorest households were favoured in the selection criteria. But what will happen if the systems are made available across the country, using a privatization and market-oriented model? It is not at all clear that low-income households will be able to afford the GW systems if market forces determine system costs to the household. Within a national policy environment favouring privatization, what policy and legal frameworks are required to ensure that universal access to water management services is maintained?

Sustainable approaches to resource definition and valuation are required

In Jordan, as in many other places, there is a strong consensus that water should be priced and some level of water management cost recovery should be required. There also has been a significant international move toward privatization of water provision and waste treatment. One issue that arises in such a discussion is the resource valuation of water prior to treatment. Accepting that water is a vital national asset and a human right, more innovative economic models are needed to equitably and effectively apportion the costs associated with sustainable water management and the economic benefits of the economic valuation assigned to water, so that the most effective model for water protection and conservation can be designed. It cannot simply be a downloading of costs onto the community and the household.

Final remarks

The road to decentralization of water management is a potentially fruitful but complex one. To date, the debate has focused on the technical and economic advantages of decentralized technologies. Examination of the case study highlights the equally important cultural, social, and political dimensions of the debate. What are the merits, possibilities, and limitations of participatory governance at the local level, and what is the relationship between the local level and the higher level of government? The Karak project highlights the need to define a new role for the professional or expert in a more decentralized (perhaps democratized) and integrated water management model.

The vision we are proposing for effective local water-management is much more profoundly integrated and collaborative than the conventional model. Partnership is a key. Roles are less rigid and more flexible as all partners define their contribution and working relationships. It is no less than a cultural evolution where many of the norms and conventions are questioned, examined, and revised. In the new paradigm, engineers get a better result by using the power of community organizers to get their water systems up, running, and maintained. Community organizers get a better result using the technologies as an entry point to empower the community and its marginalized members. The community benefits by learning how to use its newly gained power to leverage social and economic benefits. Finally, to the extent that the model works and is replicable, the nation benefits through the stability that effective water management and, ultimately, increased well-being provide for its citizens.

Acknowledgements

Financial support for this research was provided by the International Development Research Centre. We also would like to thank the people of the Al-Amer villages for their generosity, hospitality and commitment to this project.

References

Abu-Shams, I. and Rabadi, A. (2003) 'Commercialization and public-private partnership in Jordan', *Water Resources Development* 19: 159–72.

Alkhaddar, R.M., Sheehy, W.J.S. and Al-Ansari, N. (2005) 'Jordan's water resources: Supply and future demand', *Water International* 30: 294–303.

Beaumont, P. (2002) 'Water policies for the Middle East in the 21st century: The new economic realities', *Water Resources Development* 18: 315–34.

Biswas, A.K. (2001) 'Water policies in the developing world', *Water Resources Development* 17: 489–499.

Biswas, A.K. (2005) 'An assessment of future global water issues', *Water Resources Development* 21: 229–37.

Canadian International Development Agency (CIDA) (1999) *CIDA's Policy on Gender Equality*, CIDA, Hull, Canada.

Chambers, R. (1997) *Whose Reality Counts? Putting the First Last*, Intermediate Technology Publications, London.

Faruqui, N., Biswas, A. and Bino, M. (eds) (2001) *Water Management in Islam*, United Nations University Press, Tokyo.

Freire, P. (1968) *Pedagogy of the Oppressed*, Seabury Press, New York.

Mara, D.D. (1998) 'Low-cost sewerage', in M. Simpson-Hébert and S. Wood (eds), *Sanitation Promotion* [report no. WHO/EOS/98.5], pp. 249–62, World Health Organization/Water Supply and Sanitation Collaborative Council, Geneva.

PLAN:NET (2004) *Post Project Evaluation of Greywater Treatment and Reuse Project in Tafila, Jordan* [final report].

Rocky Mountain Institute (RMI) (2004) *Case Studies of Economic Analysis and Community Decision Making for Decentralized Wastewater Systems*, National Decentralized Water Resources Capacity Development Project, RMI, Snowmass, Colorado.

World Bank (2008), World Development Indicators 2008. World Bank, Washington.

World Water Congress (2005) *Ministerial Declaration* [online], available from: http://www.mofa.go.jp/policy/environment/wwf/declaration.html [accessed 7 May 2008].

World Water Congress (2006) *Declarations* [online], available from: http://www.worldwaterforum4.org.mx/home/declarations.asp?lan [accessed 7 May 2008].

United Nations (2007) *Millennium Development Goals*, available from http://www.un.org/millenniumgoals [accessed 7 May 2008]

About the authors

Dr Keough is a consultant with PLAN:NET Ltd with experience in South and Central America, Eastern Europe, Central and Southeast Asia, and most recently Jordan. He has worked on two wastewater and GW treatment and reuse projects in the Jordan Valley and Karak. He has extensive experience with participatory approaches to development and appropriate technology. He is also assistant professor of Sustainable Design, Faculty of Environmental Design, University of Calgary, Canada.
Email: nkeough@ucalgary.ca

Samira Smirat is a community development specialist, with 18 years experience and a professional focus on the social and economic empowerment of communities using participatory development methodologies.

Stan Benjamin has over 35 years of experience working in the field of international development with expertise in policy, program/project planning and management, monitoring and evaluation, institutional organization as well as community organization and development.

CHAPTER 9

Greywater use as a gender empowerment project in Tannoura, Lebanon

Nadine Haddad El-Hajj

One greywater (GW) treatment-and-use project in Lebanon has changed the beneficiaries' lives in many ways, providing recycled water for gardening and improving the beneficiaries' socioeconomic status. In Tannoura, West Bekaa, Lebanon – a remote rural town of the Bekaa Valley – where phase II of the International Development Research Centre (IDRC) funded Greywater Treatment and Use Project is being implemented (2006–2008), female beneficiaries have been more affected than their male counterparts by this project.

The project area has been classified by a 2002 World Bank survey as one of nine poverty pockets in Lebanon – the average income in Tannoura is about US$2 per person per day. The arrival of the GW treatment-and-use project in the town, in early 2006, was praised by all the residents and especially the women, since they are in charge of water management in the houses. They felt that the used water could be allocated for irrigation, would improve food security, and most importantly would save them trips for hauling water, from the polluted town spring – the town's only source of water.

However, the project turned out to have another impact on the female beneficiaries, with the visits of the female project team experts to the town becoming an event for the female beneficiaries. The female team members were perceived as examples of modernity and liberty, especially by younger women. This has positively influenced the progress of the project, especially when men were reluctant to contribute financially. In this second phase of the GW project, women proved to be a key element in the success and sustainability of the project.

Introduction

Water scarcity affects women in their daily lives, because it adds extra work to their daily activities. This problem is obvious in Tannoura, one of four Lebanese towns that the GW treatment project this chapter addresses is targeting, where the only source of water is heavily contaminated by sewage.

The Greywater Treatment and Use Project (GW project) is being implemented in the Rashaya area of Lebanon, between 2003 and 2008. Phase I of the project began in 2003 and phase II began in 2006 and will run until 2008.

Phase II includes several outputs. It includes the establishment of GW systems in 70 households of Rashaya Caza, of which 30 are located in a town called Tannoura. It also includes the distribution of seedlings and fruit trees that will be irrigated by the treated GW and will be used for home consumption, and the formation of a local users' committee for problem solving and mitigation. The project will be evaluated through a set of quantified indicators, such as number of beneficiaries with increased income, to measure the impact of the project on the beneficiaries. A baseline measurement was taken at the beginning of the project and compared to another one taken at the conclusion of the project. Since Phase I of the project showed an important impact on women beneficiaries, and since women are the main stakeholders of water demand management and are the most affected by water shortage, the project team decided to allocate an important part of the research to monitoring changes in womens' lifestyles. The aim of the project was to collect as much data as possible on the socioeconomic characteristics of the beneficiaries in the inception phase and during the progress of the project, in order to measure how the project would affect the female beneficiaries.

Methods and instruments of data collection and interpretation are presented in the first section of this chapter, followed by research findings and discussions from the first six months of the project, which describe the advantages of this project for women. There is then a discussion of how women have been engaged in empowering activities, ending with a forecast on how this project intends to improve women's status.

The object of this chapter is to demonstrate how a project that was originally tailored to improve the economic situation of the beneficiaries, turned out to be an empowering factor for the women in Tannoura.

Methodology

The first step in the progress of phase II of the project was to understand the dynamics of the community in which the project was to be implemented, and try to draw a profile of the female community and explain how gender relations work in this specific context. The task was straightforward since the project area has ethnographic, religious, and cultural backgrounds similar to those of phase I of the GW project.

In the first place, a questionnaire was prepared according to the project objectives and the required information on gender issues and socioeconomic status of the beneficiaries, to enable the compilation of baseline data and the quantification of the impact of the project on female beneficiaries. Questions included questions profiling the families, their economic resources, gender division of labour, time management, food needs, and water supply and management.

Since social data collection is a long process and in order to avoid erroneous analysis, beneficiaries were regularly visited and the data was regularly updated after each visit. Field visits were performed by the project team members once or twice a week, in order to get to know the beneficiaries, ensure adequate inclusion and enable smooth integration in the project. It was recognized that a good first impression was essential in a community tied to its traditions and hospitality roots, and where a 'faux-pas' could lead to the rejection of the project. The project team included three women, which eased the acquaintance process.

Since this phase of the project began in May 2006, the project team made around 100 visits to the 30 households involved in the project in Tannoura, over a period of eight months. Site visits had to be interrupted during the July 2006 war and post-war period when travel to the project area was impossible.

Since secondary data on the socioeconomic situation of rural communities in Lebanon is scarce, the socioeconomic profile of the community and the beneficiaries had to be drawn from the collected primary data. During the visits to the beneficiaries, team members filled out the questionnaires over casual chats, to make the questioning less formal and to bond more with the beneficiaries. They also relied on observation to evaluate the financial situation of the beneficiaries (i.e. availability of car and its model, availability of phone, appliances, status of the house, etc.) and to adjust information provided by some beneficiaries to balance any suspected exaggeration geared towards expression of need for the project.

The importance of women in the project activities was promoted from the first general meeting with the public. During that meeting, which 60 people attended, an overview of the GW concept was presented and people were invited to participate. Application forms, which included a brief questionnaire about general water demand management practices and socioeconomic status of applying families, were distributed. Seventy complete applications/questionnaires were collected by the municipality and delivered to LATA/MECTAT, the NGO designing and implementing the project. These questionnaires provided basic information about, and an overview of, the situation in the town. They also helped develop the detailed questionnaire for collecting quantitative and qualitative baseline data.

Women were always present at the interviews and men often let their wives answer questions related to water management. Perhaps, this is because women have more information on how and where water is used. However, men always answered the questions related to financial issues. Following the first visit, meetings were conducted mainly during the morning, when men were at work and women were more comfortable answering the questions.

In the first instance, sampling of pilot beneficiaries did not take place, but all the beneficiaries were interviewed for data collection. At a later stage, a group of 10 families were selected as pilot beneficiaries, and were observed in order to evaluate the impact of the project on their lives. Since there were regular visits to the project area, it was possible while monitoring the implementation of all the project activities over a 12-month period to spot and fix erroneous data, such as when men tended to exaggerate answers related to money (i.e. income and expense) in order to promote themselves as in need of financial support and therefore have more chance of being selected for the project.

Research findings and discussions

Benefits of the project to women in Tannoura

Following the implementation of phase I of the GW project in six other towns of the Rashaya area, it was found that women played a powerful role in the sustainability of the project for the following reasons.

- Women are in charge of water management at the household level, and therefore influence the quantity and the quality of the GW to be used for irrigation purposes.
- Women spend most of their time at home. Therefore if something goes wrong with the system, they are affected, especially at the kitchen when water cannot be discharged properly from the sink because of a failure in the GW treatment system or the pump. It had been noticed in phase I of the project that although it was men and young men who were trained to clean the first barrel of the treatment kit from the accumulated particulate residues, in 90 per cent of the households, women became responsible for the cleaning process towards the end of the project.
- It is the women and children's responsibility to haul water from the town spring. In Tannoura people suffer from severe water stress. Its residents have never been connected to a municipal piped-water network and the only public water spring is heavily polluted from uncontrolled sewage disposal. Women often have to carry the filled water gallons back home, either on their shoulders or by using wheel-barrows or donkeys. This activity puts strain on their backs. Thirty per cent of the interviewed women suffer from back pain problems, which is most likely due to carrying heavy water containers from the spring. It should also be noted that water brought from the town spring can be used only to wash the floor. This water is non-potable, due to its contamination with bacteria. It is men's responsibility to bring in drinking water, as they have to fill it from neighbouring towns' springs and transport it by car back home.
- In keeping with Middle Eastern culture, it is men's role to provide income for the household. However in the study area, women manage the expenses at the household level and provide food and water with the available money.
- In Tannoura during phase II of the project, women welcomed the project as soon as they became aware of it, while men had some reservations regarding the required cost-sharing. Women, therefore, contributed positively to the project by pushing their husbands to pay the required 10 per cent share of the total cost, at a time when failing to pay this share of the cost threatened to freeze the implementation of the project.

In Tannoura, 72 women aged between 15 and 80 years (30 per cent of the total beneficiary population) directly benefit from this project and have contributed to the acceptance of the project, probably because they realized its benefits, particularly in reducing their work load.

Ever since the first visits to Tannoura, women have proved to be very active and willing to contribute to the success of this project. It has to be understood that only five per cent of women are employed, and since the town is far from neighbouring towns, women spend all their free time visiting each other and watching TV, in addition to doing their household chores. The meetings between the project team and the village women acted like a window to the entire village, since the interviews were casual. Women who were not part of the project often asked to attend the meetings as well. Conversations often drifted to comparing their lives to those of the team members, especially for young women in their early twenties. A 22-year-old beneficiary, holder of an accounting diploma and engaged for the third time, told the team members, 'I wish I had your lives, I wish I could work instead of being stuck with a fiancé I can't stand'. In response to that, this young woman was trained on water-use diary keeping and was appointed to train other women on diary keeping and to monitor their regularity in registering their water-related activities and use.

Although the GW project did not provide additional freshwater for households or reduce the loads carried from the spring, it reduced women's water management chores. Indeed, most of the women use water several times before its final disposal, which adds to their workload. Data collected throughout the project showed that 30 per cent of the visited houses have their sink disconnected from the cesspit, or the septic tank, because they do not want to fill the cesspit with water that can be used again. As well as increasing water availability, this reduces the cost of emptying the cesspit. Greywater is collected in buckets and used either for irrigating trees or for toilet flushing. In Tannoura, 10 per cent of the visited houses do not have kitchens. Dishes are cleaned outside the house in buckets and 'kitchens are not needed since there is no water'.

The GW treatment-and-use system collects the used water in the treatment kits. Irrigation is later carried out automatically when an electric pump is activated and the trees are easily irrigated, via drip irrigation systems provided by the project. This reduces the extra chores (i.e. cleaning the barrels, diary keeping and group meetings) that women have to bear during the project life, and improves their acceptance of the systems.

On another level, the project offered the beneficiaries a social demarcation. Interviewed women had heard of GW technology before, but, until the implementation of the project, they felt it was reserved to richer families. Women, therefore, used the project as a 'show-off tool', which increased the demands for the systems in the village.

During the introductory meeting, women constituted 70 per cent of the audience. Men asked questions about installation procedures and women asked about requirements at the kitchen level. Twenty per cent of the beneficiaries declared that they were convinced about the importance of the project during the introductory meeting and pushed their husbands to fill the application forms.

Female beneficiaries also showed a willingness to contribute to all the activities proposed by the team, such as diary keeping and installing measurement units at their houses, because it was a form of prestige that would distinguish them from the rest of the town.

Empowering activities offered by the project

The project also offered other empowering activities, besides those listed above, for beneficiary women. These included training sessions on food processing and inclusion in the local committee for GW.

Training on food processing

Training on food processing of locally grown fruits and vegetables started in January 2007. The training was offered to all of the town residents and attendance sheets revealed that only 50 per cent of the attendees were beneficiaries of the GW project. The training was aimed at processing and preserving crops grown in backyard gardens, using traditional recipes, in order to improve the economic independence of local women. A close relationship with the Women's Cooperative for Food Processing in the neighbouring town of Rashaya has motivated these women to process their crops for income generation, after seeing a successful model that had managed to export produce to the Gulf market.

The idea of having a local committee was born during the formulation of phase II of the GW project proposal to the WaDImena initiative, based on lessons learned from phase I. This committee aimed specifically at conflict resolution among beneficiaries and non-beneficiaries in the town, especially in cases where beneficiaries refused to pay their contribution for the connection of the kits. This committee was trained in resolving such issues. The local committee, represented all the stakeholders of the town and women were highly encouraged to participate as members of the committee.

Two examples of women who were eager to participate in the committee are as follows: The first is a 30-year old housewife with two children, whose husband, a soldier, is away for most of the week. She attended the introductory meeting and believed in the project so much that she undertook the connection work while her husband was on duty, because she believed that 'he would never have refused such a vital project'. This housewife lives in the most remote house from the town spring and the entire water supply is purchased from a local vendor who pumps his water from an artesian well he dug, at a cost of US$64 per month for a family of four, living with an income of US$600 per month. She said, 'at least now I know that 10 per cent of my income does not go down the drain; I will be able to grow food for my children instead'.

The second example is an 18-year old woman who is the only source of income for her family. This woman works at the town's public school as a janitor and holds a small vending shop that was donated to her by one of the deputies of the region. She earns around US$400 per month for a family of six living in a three-room house. She proved to be a great help in the project. Ever since she was asked to join the committee, she took the job seriously, inspecting the neighbours' kits and informing the project team when abuses occurred. With a history of being an 'outcast' in the village, the GW project gave her a chance at reintegration into the society.

The local committee is an empowering tool for Tannoura's women since it is their first opportunity to participate in such a decision-making group. It is worth noting that the municipality was opposed to the idea of having a committee external to the municipality. The mayor was afraid that it would replace the municipality's role and believed that giving women authority may offend some of the more conservative people in the town. To mitigate this issue, a public meeting was called in mid-December 2006 to introduce the committee's role and mission. The meeting was a success, and beneficiaries showed interest in participating in the election and in involving women in the committee.

Phase II of the GW project ran from 2006 to 2008 and women have benefited from it. As the project progresses, more women will prove to be champions of the project, especially when the crops start to blossom and the efforts in gardening start to pay. They will be praised for setting an example for others to follow and for demonstrating to other communities the importance of GW use.

Anticipated future empowering factors

Other empowering factors are anticipated during the lifetime of the project. These will be examined according to the findings from the before and after project periods. Anticipated factors include:

- Improvement in economic conditions by allowing a reduction of expenditure, since the GW treatment-and-use system allows beneficiaries to save some money from emptying their cess-pits.
- Better dietary habits – the project includes the distribution of seeds and tree seedlings that are not usually grown in the area because they need water for irrigation. Poor families often cannot afford to consume these fruits and vegetables. Women will be happy to see their children have a balanced diet, which will be made possible by the GW project.
- Although the treated GW will not provide beneficiary women with water to clean their houses, cook, or even wash their clothes, it will reduce their number of visits to haul water from the town spring. It also offers

them a source of water to irrigate the flowers on their porches, which reflects a public image of what is regarded to be a good housewife.

Conclusions and recommendations

Phase II of the GW project, in its inception period from May to December 2006, has already proved to be an empowering agent for women in Tannoura. Throughout the project, participatory methodologies and techniques were used and women, being a major stakeholder, were included in all activities.

Weekly field visits were conducted by the three women of the project team to collect baseline data relating to water demand management, actual crop production, and socioeconomic status of beneficiaries, as well as data and observations on women's activities relating to water demand management. This data was processed to draw a profile of the community, especially women, to be able to evaluate how GW treatment and use affected their lives, economically and socially, by the end of the project.

The preliminary findings indicated that women in Tannoura are the main water managers at the household level, as they are the ones responsible for water supply and for maximising its use at the household level. This revealed the physical stress that women face in Tannoura, including back problems linked to water hauling and extra chores generated by the traditional use of water. In addition, there is an emotional stress related to water scarcity and the associated expenses. Many women cannot grow crops in their backyards, as they cannot afford to buy water for irrigation. Furthermore, the problem of wastewater disposal, which is carried out by pump trucks, adds extra charges to their limited income.

In the GW project, women found a way to alleviate some of this stress and, therefore, turned out to be prominent supporters of this project since its beginning. Indeed women proved to be a positive influence in resolving problems related to the implementation of the project, as they pressured their husbands to finalize the installation of the kits. Women also showed their support by participating in all the activities designed for them, such as interviews for data collection, group meetings, training on how to efficiently use the GW treatment-and-use kits, training workshops on food processing of locally grown crops, and participation in the local committee for the local management and conflict resolution.

The local committee is the main empowering tool for Tannoura's women, since it gave them the chance to participate in decision making activities. Two women have already volunteered to participate in the committee as members and they have already started helping the team members by reporting any technical problem or abuse at the beneficiaries' houses.

Other empowering factors are predicted and will be proven by the end of the project as more data is collected and analysed. These are expected to include improvement in economic status, in dietary habits for the whole family, and in the social image of the households. In the long run, it is hoped that this greywater project will help reduce women's back problems.

So far women have proved to be a key to the success factor of the GW project in Lebanon. Since rural women in the Middle East and North Africa region share more or less the same characteristics in gender issues and water management, it is recommended to use a SAGA (social and gender analysis) approach in future water-related projects and to consider women as the main stakeholder to ensure the sustainability of greywater projects.

Related resources

Hovorka, A. (1998) *Gender Resources for Urban Agriculture Research: Methodology, Directory and Annotated Bibliography*, International Development Research Centre (IDRC), Cities Feeding People (CFP) Series, Report no. 26, Ottawa.

Nabulo, G., Nasinyama, G. and Oryem-Origa, H. (2004) 'The role of women in urban food production and food security in Kampala City, Uganda', *Women Feeding Cities Workshop: Gender Mainstreaming in Urban Food Production and Food Security* [online], Resource Centres on Urban Agriculture and Food Security (RUAF), Accra, Ghana, available from http://www.ruaf.org/sites/default/files/gender_nabulo_kampala_final_version.pdf [accessed 18 January 2009].

Nations Unis (2002) *La féminisation de la pauvreté dénoncée devant la Commission de la condition de la femme*, Commission de la condition de la femme, Nation Unis.

The World Bank 'Promising approaches to engendering development' [online], available from: http://siteresources.worldbank.org/INTGENDER/Resources/IndonesiaCDDPromisingApproach.pdf [accessed 18 January 2009].

The World Bank (2001) 'Engendering development through gender equality in rights, resources, and voice' [online]. available from: http://www-wds.worldbank.org/external/default/WDSContentServer/WDSP/IB/2001/03/01/000094946_01020805393496/Rendered/PDF/multi_page.pdf [accessed 5 February 2009].

The World Bank (2002) 'Integrating gender into the World Bank's work: A strategy for action' [online]. available from http://siteresources.worldbank.org/INTGENDER/Resources/strategypaper.pdf [accessed 18 January 2009].

The World Bank (2006) 'Gender equality as smart economics: A World Bank Group Gender Action Plan (fiscal years 2007–10)' [online]. available from http://siteresources.worldbank.org/INTGENDER/Resources/GAPNov2.pdf [accessed 18 January 2009].

United Nations (UN) (2006) 'The millennium development goals report' [online], UN, New York, available from: http://mdgs.un.org/unsd/mdg/Resources/Static/Products/Progress2006/MDGReport2006.pdf [accessed 18 January 2009].

United Nations Educational, Scientific and Cultural Organization (UNESCO) (2005) 'Education for sustainable development information brief' [online], UNESCO, Paris, available from http://portal.unesco.org/education/en/files/30372/11035297673brief_Gender.pdf/brief%2BGender.pdf [accessed 5 February 2009].

Vernooy, R. (ed.) (2006) *Social and gender analysis in natural resource management: Learning Studies and Lessons from Asia*, Sage, Thousand Oaks.
Web site of the Division for the Advancement of Women, Department of Economic and Social Affairs, United Nations: http://www.un.org/womenwatch/daw/daw/ [accessed 5 February, 2009]
World Health Organisation (WHO) (2006) *Guidelines for the Safe Use of Wastewater, Excreta and Greywater* (vols 1–4), WHO, Geneva.

About the author

Nadine Haddad El-Hajj works for the Beeatoona Organization, a Lebanese non-governmental organization formed in 2008, whose primary aim is the promotion of sustainable development and good environmental practices among Lebanese and Arab communities. She holds a postgraduate diploma in Rural Environment Development from the Agronomic Mediterranean Institute of Saragossa, Spain.
Email: nadinelhajj@gmail.com

CHAPTER 10
Greywater use: Islamic perspectives

Odeh Rashed Al-Jayyousi

This chapter aims to address some Islamic perspectives and principles relating to greywater (GW) use and to justify and explain the value of GW use as a part of an integrated water resource management (IWRM) approach from an Islamic perspective. The chapter outlines a set of Islamic principles that argue for the practice of GW use as a means of sound water and agriculture management. These principles include the concepts of waste, innovation (ijtihad), continuous improvement (ihsan), public interest (maslaha) and proportion (mizan).

The chapter uses Islamic principles to recommend a new approach to link conservation and culture, by developing a new consciousness towards the role of the human as a trustee (shahid) of nature. This role is believed to be a key to ensuring an active system of human–environmental security that limits and controls all forms of mischief (fasad).

Background

A number of studies have dealt with Islamic principles relating to the management of natural resources. Ba Kader and others (1983) argued that the concept of conservation in Islam needs to be embodied in natural resources management and planning. Izz al Din (1990) held that Islamic environmental ethics is divinely derived and that Islamic law (*shari'a*) contains legal and ethical principles that are interconnected. Farooq and Ansari (1981) and Abderrahman (2001) found that an Islamic approach to recycling wastewater could serve as a useful background to discuss and promote wastewater recycling in Islamic countries.

Elsewhere, I reviewed and explored the relationship between Islam and the Dublin Principles on water management. I argued that Islam provides a holistic and comprehensive framework for the management of resources, which ensures equity, efficiency and sustainability (Al-Jayyousi, 2001). Faruqui and others (2001) highlighted the role of local knowledge in informing water management.

It is imperative to shed some light on the broad concepts and fundamentals of Islam, in order to see the convergence between water management and Islamic principles. Islam offers a new worldview towards humanity, nature and the built environment. This is not limited to the confined domain of religion and spirituality (the relation between man and God), but rather offers a comprehensive approach to understanding all aspects of life. Islam offers a holistic framework for looking at the cosmos and nature and it strives to define both purpose and value for the human being. For example, contemporary Islam has contextualized a number of economic institutions (Islamic banking and *waqf* funds) and social institutions (health care and education). It would be of value to outline the basic principles that demonstrate and justify the value of GW use. This means that water management will not only be informed by culture and local knowledge, but also can be developed and transformed by Islam, through the process of reconstruction of knowledge and the revival of the human consciousness.

The key characteristic of Islam is the belief in one God (*Allah*) and the belief in the Day of Judgement. These form the core of social and environmental responsibility for both individuals and the corporate sector. Consciousness about the role of the human as a trustee and a witness (*shahid*) raises the sense of responsibility for individuals, organizations and societies to mange resources (including water) in a sustainable manner. Islam teaches that nature is created by *Allah* for the benefit of humans. The relationship between the human and nature is based on harmony, since all creatures obey the laws (*sunan*) of God. Humans are urged to explore and utilize natural resources in a sustainable manner. Harmonization of human's will with the teachings of Islam leads to a responsible, balanced and good life (*haya tayabah*). Being mindful of the purpose and meaning of every single human endeavour, each human activity is given a transcendent dimension; it becomes meaningful, of value, and goal-centred. Islam provides a balance for the components or the four capitals of *sustainable development* (this author uses the term *tayabah development*). These include the natural capital (the environment), social capital (people), manufactured capital (technology) and financial capital (economics) (Hawken et al., 2002).

At the legal-framework level, some basic Islamic principles are fixed (*thabit*) and others are changeable (*mutaghayyir*) in response to changing conditions. This implies that a general framework and guiding principles are defined, but that specific details and applications may vary to respond to the changing needs of life. In Islam, the main source of ruling is jurisprudence (*shari'a*), which is based on both Quran (as revelation) and the Prophet's sayings and acts (*sunna*). However, these sources of passing judgments are by no means exhaustive. One other fundamental source for devising rulings is innovation (*ijtihad*), which means the striving to develop new laws, rules and judgments to address and respond to changing conditions.

The basic methods of understanding, interpreting and devising new rules (after Quran and Hadith) include the following:

- Analogy or relevance (*qiyas*). Islamic scholars are entitled to pass judgments on new events or issues by making analogies from historical incidents through personal reasoning and interpretation.

- Unanimous agreement of the jurists (*ijma'*). *Ijma'* can refer to either the consensus of the whole community or the consensus of the religious authorities regarding the interpretation of a Quranic text or Tradition, or a development of legal principle. For example, the general consensus of Muslim jurists (*fuqaha'*) has always been that the *shari'a* is concerned with human welfare and based on justice and equity.
- Juristic preference (*istihsan*). In cases where no ruling exists, judgments may be based on the common preference of jurists.
- Public interest or human welfare (*maslaha*). If none of the above means of passing judgment exist, the collective benefit of society or public interest is considered as a means to devise new rulings.
- Continuance or permanence (*istishab*).

These rules and principles will now be used to develop a framework to deal with water management issues that is informed by Islam (Faruqui and Al-Jayyousi, 2001).

The Islamic worldview is based on an eco-cosmic understanding of the harmony between human and nature and the value of nurturing the aesthetic and natural intelligence of humans as trustees of nature. The Islamic notion of *zuhd* – 'living lightly on earth', as explained in the set of Hadiths by Prophet Muhammad (Al-Emam Al-Nawawi, 1992: 230), and having a low ecological footprint – is a key for securing a healthy planet. All forms of environmental problems such as pollution, global warming, and climate change, can be attributed to human misconduct or mischief (*fasad*), according to Islamic interpretation.

The *shari'a* stipulates the law of God and provides guidance for the regulation of life in the best interests of humans and the natural environment. Its objective is to show the best route to human wellbeing and livelihood. To achieve this goal, there should be mutual assistance and cooperation among human beings. Islam regards knowledge and science as the common heritage of humankind. Muslims have both the freedom and obligation to learn from other cultures. This assimilation of knowledge and wisdom (*hikma*) is a key to the transformation and enlightenment of society. 'Wisdom is sought by a believer; wherever he finds it, he makes use of it' (Al-Tirmidhi: Hadith no. 2687). In light of the above Islamic notions and concepts, a set of GW-use principles will now be devised.

Islamic principles for greywater use

The following is a set of principles for GW use outlined based on Islamic concepts and informed by Islam.

Principle 1: Greywater is not a waste but a resource

Islam does not allow waste among even lifeless things, to the extent that it disapproves of the wasteful use of water, even where there is no scarcity of water. It teaches the avoidance of waste in every conceivable form and requires making the best use of all resources. Islam, therefore, reforms the notion of 'waste' and enlightens the human mind to rethink the concept of waste by learning from nature and ecological processes. Also, Islam urges conservation of resources and living lightly on earth (*zuhd*). It is stated in both Quran and Hadith that waste in all forms is unacceptable. The Prophet ordered not to waste water even when washing for prayers (performing ablution). Quran says, 'But waste not by excess: for Allah loveth not the wasters' (6:141).

Greywater is usually wash water – bath, dish and laundry water, excluding toilet and food wastes. When dealt with appropriately, GW can be a valuable resource for horticulture, agriculture and home gardening uses. Some chemical components of GW – i.e. phosphorous, potassium and nitrogen – are excellent sources of nutrition to plants.

Dish, shower, basin and laundry water comprise 50–80 per cent of residential wastewater and may be used for landscape irrigation. The benefits of GW recycling include the reduction of freshwater use, effective purification, groundwater recharge and plant growth. GW use can therefore be incorporated into an ecological design.

For waste with different qualities like GW and saline water, Islam in Quran instructs the mind that regardless of the quality of water, whether it is fresh ('*adhb*) or saline (*milh 'ujaj*), it can be of use and value for many purposes: a food source from sea fishing, a source for jewellery and ornaments from sea species like oysters – which was a business for early coastal and hydraulic civilizations – and a means for shipping, trade, and transport.

> And not alike are the two seas.
> One is fresh and sweet, palatable for drinking, and one that is salty and bitter. And from each you eat tender meat and extract ornaments which you wear, and you see the ships plowing through (them) that you might seek of his bounty; and so as to be thankful (Quran, 5:12).

By interpretation, and using the notion of public interest (*maslaha*), it is safe to say that GW and wastewater can be of use and value to humans if treated with proper processes. This was confirmed by a judgment and ruling (*fatwa*) by Muslim scholars from different disciplines who confirmed that wastewater can be appropriate for human use if treated properly (Abderrahman, 2001). The *fatwa*, issued in 1978 by the Council of Leading Islamic Scholars (CLIS) in Saudi Arabia, postulated that:

> Impure waste water can be considered as pure water and similar to the original pure water, if its treatment using advanced technical procedures is capable of removing impurities with regard to taste, colour and smell, as witnessed by honest, specialized and knowledgeable experts. Then it can be

used to remove body impurities and for purifying, even for drinking (cited in *Journal of Islamic Research* 17: 40–41).

Principle 2: Greywater use requires appropriate technology and innovation (ijtihad) and continuous improvement (ihsan)

Ijtihad implies the continuous striving to innovate and enhance people's ability to harness technology, to accept institutional change, and to adapt to new contexts. Responding to local needs and utilizing local resources to develop cost-effective and appropriate solutions are key concepts in Islam, and referred to as *ihsan*.

Principle 3: Apply the precautionary principle to ensure sustainability and human security

Islamic rulings devised clear guidance with respect to managing risks, costs and tradeoffs. Islamic law stipulates that there is a role for public policy and government to secure a common welfare and to eliminate injuries to society. The limits of such interference are defined in Islamic public policy by the ultimate purposes of Islamic legislation.

In Islam, all acts are evaluated in terms of their consequences as social good and benefits (*masalih*) and social detriment (*mafasid*). Muslim planners, designers and policy makers must always aim for the universal common good of all created beings. This means that they must strive to harmonize and fulfil all interests. However, when it is impossible to satisfy all immediate interests, the universal common good requires evaluation and prioritization by weighing the welfare of the greatest number, the importance and urgency of the various interests involved, the certainty or probability of benefit or injury, and the ability of those affected to secure their interests without assistance.

In light of the above notions, these basic principles have been articulated and documented in the *IUCN Environmental Policy and Law Paper No. 20* (1994: 18–21).

- The interests of the society as a whole take priority over the interests of individuals and various groups when they cannot be reconciled. Among the Juristic principles of Islamic law are: 'Priority is given to preserving the universal interest over particular interests', and '[t]he general welfare takes priority over individual welfare'. From this basis is derived the principle that '[a] private injury is accepted to avert a general injury to the public'. Similarly, sacrificing private interest for the purpose of achieving and protecting the common interest of the public is related to the juristic principles that '[t]he lesser of two harms (*darar*) shall be chosen', '[s]evere damage shall be removed by means of lighter damage' and '[i]f one of two opposing detriments is unavoidable, the more injurious is averted by the commission of the less injurious'.

- Consideration is to be given to the abilities of various groups to secure their welfare without the government's intervention. The governing authorities are obliged to protect and care for the disadvantaged and less influential groups in accordance with the juristic principles that '[t]he averting of harm from the poor takes priority over the averting of harm from the wealthy' and '[t]he welfare of the poor takes priority over the welfare of the wealthy'.
- Some actions may help to achieve certain interests, but unavoidably bring about damage and destruction of similar or even greater magnitude. The juristic principle in this connection is that '[t]he averting of harm takes precedence over the acquisition of benefits', for indeed the first step towards the achievement and realization of the common good is to eliminate damage and destruction.

The use of GW in agriculture and its role in poverty alleviation is documented by Faruqui and Al-Jayyousi (2002) and Al-Jayyousi (2004). These precautionary principles provide useful insights and guidance to GW use.

Principle 4: Realizing benefits from greywater use requires sound maintenance, care for natural resources, and the avoidance of externalities

Greywater use at both community- and household-level provides a useful means of advancing human wellbeing and livelihood. It is evident that there is a benefit and a public interest in using GW. To ensure sustainable benefits, it is imperative to limit and control negative impacts from GW use. The *IUCN Policy and Law Paper No. 20* (1994) outlined specific guidance with respect to benefits from natural resources, as will be discussed below.

In Islam, the right to benefit from the essential environmental elements and resources, such as water, rangeland, fire and other sources of energy, forests, fish and wildlife, arable soil, air, and sunlight, is a right held in common by all members of society. Such benefits may be direct – by way of harvesting or extracting the resource – or indirect by way of access to its products. Each individual is entitled to benefit from a common resource to the extent of his need, so long as he does not violate, infringe, or delay the equal rights of other members. In return for profiting from the GW use, beneficiaries are obliged to maintain its original value. If they cause its destruction, impairment, or degradation, they will be held liable to the extent of repairing the damage, because they have violated the rights of every member of society.

Principle 5: Greywater use is to be allocated to appropriate uses, based on water quality and level of treatment

Islam teaches that 'everything is created from water' and that water at the global level is finite (*biqadr*) and is in balance (*mawzoon*). Also, Islam believes that water should be allocated to different uses with priority to water for drinking (*haq al shafa*). Greywater can be used for different types of irrigation based on the level of treatment and quality of it.

Islam also recognizes a certain 'right of the environment' in regard to water. The emphasis on balance, conservation, and harmony is key to the Islamic view of water use (Caponera, 1973, 1992). According to Mallat (1995), there are clear priorities for water allocation in Islam. Water for drinking has first priority, followed by the water rights for cattle. Third priority is given to irrigation needs, as well as environmental (ecological) needs. For example, animals have rights to sufficient water of good quality (Caponera, 1992).

In terms of sharing water resources and definition of common pool resources, Islam teaches that water, fire (fuel) and grass are public goods. The Prophet declared that free access to public water is the right of the community (ibid). The Prophet stated that '[p]eople are partners in three resources: water, pasture, and fire' (Ibn Majah after Ibn Abbas in Zuhaily, 1989).

If water, wastewater or GW resources are developed and conveyed to people, the government can charge the cost of development and operation. Zuhaily (1989) concluded that individuals and groups have the right to use, sell, and recover the value-added costs of most types of water.

Conclusion and recommendations

There are two salient features of the Islamic model for sustainable natural resource. First, knowledge can be attained through revelation (this is the belief systems and basics) and through human reasoning, experimentation and innovation (*ijtihad*). Second, the human being is considered as a trustee and a witness who is responsible for the 'construction of the world' ('*imarat al-kawn*), not as a consumer who intends to exploit nature. Humans have been endowed with countless powers and faculties. They possess intellect and wisdom to achieve balance in this universe. God also provided humans with all the means and resources to make their natural faculties function and to achieve the fulfilment of their needs. The environment contains resources that humans can harness. Islam teaches that human beings should cooperate and exchange knowledge and wisdom (*hikma*) with other nations to establish a better and prosperous life. Such proper use of humanity's powers leads to the attainment of benefits to the general public. Every other use of resources that results in waste or destruction is wrong and unreasonable.

An Islamic perspective on natural resource management provides the right balance between the economic, social, and environmental agendas and discourses. Also, it can help create a new social contract between public, private, and community stakeholders, with respect to the allocation of water in an equitable and sustainable manner.

A set of principles for GW use has been derived from Islamic principles. Such principles urge policy makers and professionals to employ all possible means at all levels to call all individuals to commit themselves to Islamic ethics, morals, and manners when dealing with nature, the environment, and the natural resources. All individuals should ensure sustainable development of the Earth and its resources, elements, and phenomena. This can be achieved through the enhancement of natural resources, the protection and conservation of resources as well as all existing forms of life, and the bringing of new life to the land through its reclamation and the rehabilitation and purification of the soil, air, and water.

References

Abderrahman, W.A. (2001) 'Water demand management in Saudi Arabia', in N. Faruqi, A. Biswas and M. Bino (eds.), *Water Management in Islam*, pp. 68–78, United Nations University Press, Tokyo.

Al-Emam Al-Nawawi (1992) *Riyad Assaliheen* [in Arabic], rev. M.N. Al-Albani, Al-Maktab Al-Islami, Beirut.

Al-Jayyousi, O.R. (2001) 'Islamic water management and the Dublin Statement', in N. Faruqi, A. Biswas and M. Bino (eds), *Water Management in Islam*, pp. 33–8, United Nations University Press, Tokyo.

Al-Jayyousi, O.R. (2004) 'Greywater reuse: knowledge management for sustainability', *Desalination* 167: 27–37.

Al-Tirmidhi (comp.) and Abu-Hurayra (narrator), 'Prophet Muhammad's Sayings', in *Kitab Al-'Ilm* [in Arabic].

Ba Kader, A., Al Sabagh, A., Al Glenid, M. and Izz al Din, M. (1983) 'Islamic principles for the conservation of natural environment', in *IUCN Environmental Policy and Law Paper No. 20 Rev.*, International Union for the Conservation of Nature (IUCN) and the Meteorological Protection Administration of the Kingdom of Saudi Arabia, Gland, Switzerland.

Caponera, D.A. (1973) 'Water laws in Muslim countries', *Irrigation and Drainage Paper No 20/1*, Food and Agriculture Organization of the United Nations (FAO), Rome.

Caponera, D.A. (1992) *Principles of Water Law and Administration: National and International*, Balkema Publishers, Rotterdam.

Council of Leading Islamic Scholars (CLIS) (1978) 'Judgement regarding purifying wastewater', Judgement no. 64 on 25 Shawwal 1398 AH, *13th Meeting of the Council of Leading Islamic Scholars*, Taif, Saudi Arabia.

Farooq, S. and Ansari, Z. (1981) 'Philosophy of Water Reuse: An Islamic Perspective: Water – The Essence of Life', *Proceedings of the International Congress on Desalination and Water Re-use*, Manama.

Faruqi, N., Biswas, A. and Bino, M. (eds) (2001) *Water Management in Islam*, United Nations University Press, Tokyo.

Faruqi, N. and Al-Jayyousi, O.R. (2001) 'Islamic sources', in N. Faruqi, A. Biswas and M. Bino (eds), *Water Management in Islam*, pp. xx–xxii, United Nations University Press, Tokyo.

Faruqi, N. and Al-Jayyousi, O. (2002) 'Greywater reuse in urban agriculture for poverty alleviation: A case study from Jordan', *Water International* 27: 387–94.

Hawken, P., Lovins, A.B. and Lovins, L.H. (2002) *Natural Capitalism: The Next Industrial Revolution*, Earthscan, London.

IUCN–The World Conservation Union (1994) *IUCN Environmental Policy and Law Paper No. 20: Environmental Protection in Islam*, 2nd edn, pp. 18–20, IUCN, Gland, Switzerland.

Izz al Din, M.Y. (1990) 'Islamic environmental ethics, law and society', in J.R. Engel and J.G. Engel (eds), *Ethics of Environment and Development: Global Challenges and International Response*, pp. 189–98, University of Arizona Press, Tucson.

Mallat, C. (1995) 'The quest for water use principles: reflections on the shari'a and custom in the Middle East', in J.A. Allan, C. Mallat, S. Wade and J. Wild (eds), *Water in the Middle East: Legal, Political, and Commercial Implications*, pp. 127–38, I.B. Tauris, New York.

Zuhaily, W. (1989) *Al-Fiqh Al-Islami wa Dalalatuh* – part 4 [in Arabic], 3rd edn, Dar Al-Fikr, Beirut.

About the author

Dr Al-Jayyousi is the regional director for West Asia/Middle East regional office, IUCN. He served as a university professor in water resources and environment and dean of scientific research at the Applied Science University, Jordan. His research interest is in the domain of water policy and sustainable development.
E-mail: odeh.al.jayyousi@iucn.org

PART III
Policy issues and next steps

CHAPTER 11
Policy and regulatory approaches to greywater use in the Middle East

Stephen McIlwaine

This chapter looks at the need for comprehensive water-use policies that address greywater (GW) and argues for a regulatory approach which is both effective and workable. Regulatory approaches to GW use adopted in the US and Australia are examined to determine how the balance is made between practical and cost-effective GW use, and risk management. The context of the MENA region is discussed, together with some key elements that locally derived policies should address.

Introduction: The need for policy

Previous chapters have asserted that the countries of the MENA region have to address increasing water demand in the context of increasingly over-exploited water resources. As countries consider non-conventional water sources to supplement their supplies, GW use is one option that is gaining interest from both consumers and policy makers. Studies such as CSBE (2003), Burnat and Eshtayah (Chapter 2), Suleiman and colleagues (Chapter 4), and Bino and others in this volume (Chapter 3) have shown that particularly water-stressed households and communities are reusing their household GW, regardless of the legality or health risks. However, such informal GW use often does not adequately manage the risks to health and the environment, leaving water-stressed, low-income populations facing additional health problems.

Despite the research efforts on the technical aspects of GW use, the piloting of a number of systems suitable to the MENA region as described in earlier chapters, and the promotion of GW use, especially among low-income rural communities, by donor organizations such as the International Development Research Centre (IDRC), government policies on promoting and regulating GW use are not adequately developed. Countries adopting centrally managed combined wastewater use have been hesitant to promote GW use, partly since it reduces the amount of wastewater reaching the treatment plants. Governments are wary of allowing too much decentralized control of GW because of health risks. No state has taken a clear view of the financial and economic benefits of GW use in comparison with the alternatives. Even where there is an appreciation of the worth of GW, no MENA country has developed a clear approach to its use that clearly states the responsibilities of the users and the regulatory requirements. There is a need for policy and regulatory frameworks in the region to be examined in order to harmonize GW policy with the wider water and water-reuse policies and to encourage authorities to send out consistent messages on GW with clear rules and regulations to ensure that the required protection to health, water resources, and the environment is provided, while allowing communities to make use of this valuable resource.

The purpose of a policy

During the 2007 Experts Meeting in Aqaba, there was a realization that despite several pilot projects demonstrating the feasibility and potential of GW use, there was a general lack of policy support in the MENA countries. It seems that no country in the region has a GW code or a regulation that explicitly permits GW use and regulates it clearly, without placing undue burden on the operators. At first glance, this may seem odd in such a water-stressed region. Various reasons contribute to this, not least how relatively recently GW use has become accepted. Another factor is the region-wide tendency towards centralization and a fear that allowing decentralized, household or community managed wastewater use (even if it is only GW) brings risks that the authorities are powerless to manage.

A policy on GW should therefore seek to manage the various risks associated with its use. Risks to the health of householders, workers and consumers of produce must be addressed. Risks to the environment also must be considered. However, as well as examining and controlling risk, policy should also recognize the potential benefits of allowing GW use. The risk–benefit relationship will be different in different areas, as will the cost–benefit ratio, and each of these must be interpreted within the particular social and socioeconomic context. Policies should take into account the different contexts and should develop a clear message to households, communities and potential GW users.

When considering policy responses to the push for more GW use, the first question to ask is 'should greywater use be permitted at all?' Policy makers may decide that central control of wastewater is the best option and that the risks of household GW use are too high. Also, while it may be reasonable for authorities to prohibit GW use in urban areas – particularly areas of high population density where there is insufficient area to use the GW in irrigation – it may be more difficult to argue against allowing it in rural areas, particularly given the abundant evidence (cited earlier) that water-stressed communities are already using GW. Also, decision makers could argue that water is a commodity that has been paid for by the householder and that the government has little claim on what the householder should do with that water. If consumers choose to water their own garden with water from their own shower, which they have already purchased, it is difficult to argue that this should be prohibited.

Some commentators see the need for GW use as the result of a failure of water delivery service (either due to resource constraints, operational inefficiencies, or policy reasons like allocation). However, in the current context of the water-scarce countries in the Middle East, it is difficult to argue against facilitating and allowing decentralized, household GW use, at least in areas where there is sufficient planted area to make use of it. If central wastewater collection networks were to become widespread and provide usable water easily and cheaply to householders, then there would be arguments for prohibiting household GW use, to allow all the wastewater resource to be captured and treated centrally.

Regulatory approaches in other countries

Several formal policies on GW use have been adopted in different countries outside the MENA region. These have been reviewed in CSBE (2003), Oasis Design (2005) and Lighthouse (2007). The US states of California and Arizona provide two particularly interesting approaches. The World Health Organization (WHO) has also produced guidance on managing risk from wastewater, including GW. A selection of relevant policies and guidance is discussed below.

The 1989 WHO Health Guidelines for the Use of Wastewater in Agriculture and Aquaculture

These guidelines on the safe use of wastewater in agriculture were designed to protect agricultural workers and consumers from health risks arising from exposure to pathogens in wastewater. The approach taken focused on setting allowable concentrations of pathogens in the wastewater. These have been used as a basis for policy development in a number of developing countries, including in the MENA region.

The guidelines relate to the use of wastewater – i.e. combined black and grey wastewater – in agriculture. Although these guidelines have often been applied to GW, the risks from GW use are not the same as the risks from combined wastewater and these guidelines are therefore conservative for GW. They focus on the water quality of the wastewater that is applied to crops, emphasizing treatment as the main means to mitigate risk, and do not take into account other ways to reduce the risk. As discussed in Redwood's introduction to this volume, other risk mitigation using irrigation practices and timing, worker protection, and washing and cooking of the irrigated crops are not addressed in the guidelines. Many countries pass guidelines, but are not able to monitor or adequately enforce them. Experience has shown that a regulatory regime that focuses only on establishing guidelines for the quality of the treated GW in countries with weak monitoring capability will not have sufficient control over the output (Mara and Kramer, 2008; Redwood, 2008).

The 2006 WHO Guidelines for the Safe Use of Wastewater, Excreta and Greywater

WHO has since published a revised set of guidelines, for the Safe Use of Wastewater, Excreta and Greywater. which are based on overall risk reduction, not just control of water quality. They recognize that the risk to health from contaminated water can be controlled by means other than reducing the concentration of contaminants. Risk-control factors can include how the water is handled, how it is applied to the crops, how the crops are handled and how the end product is prepared for eating. For example, if irrigation is by an underground drip system, the risk to the agricultural workers is reduced, regardless of the quality of the water. If the crops are washed in clean water during food preparation, then the health risk to the end user is again reduced. These guidelines – discussed in more detail in the introduction – can serve as a basis for developing countries to develop their own more specific regulations, based on context.

California

The California Greywater Code – CAC (Title 24, Part 5, Appendix J, *Greywater Systems for Single Family Dwellings*) regulates GW by prescribing system designs. The code defines GW as untreated wastewater that has not come into contact with toilet waste, but can include wastewater from bathtubs, showers, bathroom wash basins, clothes washing machines, and laundry tubs, or others as approved by the local authority. The code does not allow wastewater from kitchen sinks, photo lab sinks, dishwashers, or laundry water from soiled diapers to be considered as GW.

The code mandates that all GW systems must discharge into subsurface irrigation systems and it sets procedures for estimating GW discharge volumes and for determining the irrigation capacity of the soil. The code requires soil percolation tests and/or soil analyses as the basis for determining the required area of 'disposal'. This code also sets standards for GW subsurface drip irrigation systems. The householder must therefore provide significant information to the local authority before a permit is issued. Residents in California are prohibited from applying GW above the land surface or discharging it directly into storm sewers or any body of water. In addition, humans must not come into contact with GW, except as required to maintain the treatment and distribution system, and GW must not be used for irrigating vegetable gardens.

The code has been criticized (for example, in Oasis Design (2005)) for not allowing flexibility and innovation on the part of the user. The application and permitting requirements act as a disincentive to GW use. The information and monitoring requirements imply high transactions costs for both users and agencies.

Arizona

In 2001, the Arizona Department of Environmental Quality published regulations for residential GW use. These regulations follow an interesting three-tiered approach whereby: 1) systems using under 1,500 litres per day are covered by a general permit without the need for the householder to apply for anything, provided they meet a list of reasonable conditions; 2) systems producing over 1,500 litres per day require a permit; 3) those over 13,000 litres per day are dealt with on a case-by-case basis. In these regulations, GW is defined as wastewater collected separately from clothes washers, bathtubs, showers and sinks. Use of wastewater from a kitchen sink, dishwasher, or toilet is specifically prohibited, although a revision permitting the use of kitchen sink water under certain conditions may be made in the future. Individual counties and municipalities in Arizona have passed local ordinances requiring all new homes to be constructed with GW plumbing, but leaving the decision to use GW onsite or discharge it to the sewer system up to the homeowner. Particularly in the southern part of the state (the City of Tucson, and the Counties of Pima, Santa Cruz, and Cochise) there is a growing local movement of GW use and rooftop rainwater harvesting. However, it should be noted that the water and wastewater utilities have expressed some concern that widespread adoption may lead to reduced wastewater flows at the treatment plants, thereby limiting ambitious effluent use plans.

The conditions set down for the private residential use of GW stipulate the avoidance of human contact between GW and soil irrigated by it, containment of GW from a particular residence within the property boundary, and GW usage only for household gardening. In addition, surface application of GW may not be used for irrigation of food plants, except for fruit trees, and irrigation should be restricted to flood or drip irrigation. Sprinkling is prohibited. The GW should not contain water used to wash diapers or similarly soiled or infectious garments, unless the GW is disinfected before irrigation. Likewise, the GW should not contain hazardous chemicals, for example from cleaning car parts, washing greasy or oily rags, or disposing waste solutions from home photo labs or similar hobby or home occupational activities.

The regulations require that GW systems be constructed so that if blockage, plugging, or backup of the system occurs, GW can be directed into the sewage collection system or an on-site wastewater treatment system. The GW system can include a means of filtration to reduce plugging and extend the system's lifetime. Storage tanks should be covered to restrict access and to discourage breeding of mosquitoes. The GW system should not be sited in a floodway and should be operated to maintain a minimum vertical separation distance of at least 1.5 m from the point of application to the top of the seasonally high groundwater table. Residences with an on-site wastewater treatment facility for blackwater must not change the design, capacity, or reserve area requirements for this facility if installing a GW system. Any pressure piping used that may be susceptible to cross connection with a potable water system should clearly indicate that the piping does not carry potable water.

These regulations are risk-based and widely regarded as progressive (Oasis Design, 2005). The tiered approach makes use easy for the ordinary householder and allows for innovation and flexibility of design. They do not prescribe particular design specifics and follow a performance-based approach, while the blanket prohibitions increase the protection of human and plant health.

Other US states

New Mexico has a GW law that is similar in approach to that of Arizona. As of March 2003, householders are able to install legal GW systems without applying for a permit. Provided the system meets a short list of reasonable requirements that are similar to those in the Arizona laws, it is permissible to install a GW system under one blanket permit for the whole state. Other US states, such as Texas, Nevada, Massachusetts, and Washington State, permit the use of GW under different conditions.

Queensland, Australia

The State of Queensland published guidelines (Queensland, 2008) allowing GW to be diverted from laundries and bathrooms by one of the following means: 1) manual transfer of untreated GW; 2) connecting a hose to a washing machine outlet; 3) seeking council approval for the installation of a GW diversion device or GW treatment plant. The use of kitchen wastewater is prohibited. Untreated GW must not be stored and when the immediate use of GW is not practical it is to be diverted to the sewerage system.

These guidelines allow the installation of GW diversion devices and filters that screen out hair, lint and other solids. Devices must be fitted with a switch to divert GW to a subsurface or surface irrigation system. The GW system must also automatically divert to the sewer if there is a blockage. Installation of diversion devices must be by a licensed plumber and there is an overall requirement that the GW must not cause a danger, health risk, or nuisance through ponding or run-off on to neighbouring properties. Underground irrigation systems are therefore more likely to be compliant.

Greywater treatment plants are also addressed and these can be installed in sewered and unsewered areas. In this case, the Queensland Plumbing and Wastewater Code indicates the level of treatment required for a particular end use. Approved end uses for treated GW include: 1) toilet flushing; 2) laundry use (cold water source to washing machines); 3) vehicle washing; 4) path and wall wash down; 5) lawn and garden spray irrigation.

Restrictions on the use of GW in commercial premises were lifted in January 2008, and commercial buildings can now also use GW. However, nationwide regulations[1] state that all domestic wastewater – faecal matters, urine, household slops, liquid wastes from sinks, baths and all similar fixtures – must be disposed of into the sewer system, if there is one. Greywater use therefore is still technically only permitted in non-sewered areas where it is regulated by state and local government health acts. In Queensland, the installation of any GW system, including those intended for toilet and urinal flushing, must first be authorized by the regulatory authorities.

Jordan

Jordan is one MENA country with a progressive policy towards wastewater use. The policy requires wastewater to be managed as a resource rather than a waste (MWI, 1996), and Jordan's wastewater treatment plants are gradually being upgraded to provide effluent of a quality sufficient for use. The wastewater treatment plant in Aqaba has the first tertiary treatment process in the region, with the effluent supplying landscaping irrigation water via the city's reuse water plumbing network. There is a Jordanian Standard for the use of wastewater, based on the 1989 WHO guidelines, which has varying water quality requirements, depending on the end use.

The position regarding the use of GW in Jordan is unclear. The regulation governing household plumbing is the Sanitary Wastewater System Code, (Ministry of Public Works and Housing, 1988). This provides guidelines for internal and external drainage and wastewater systems and includes extensive design guidelines for septic tanks. There is no explicit prohibition of the installation of a separate plumbing system for GW. On the contrary, it is recommended that the toilet, bidet and urinals be separated from the floor drains and sinks, until outside the building – a useful enabler for subsequent GW use. However, the code requires that 'all wastewater should be discharged using a sanitary wastewater system in accordance with the recommendations laid down in the code', and prohibits wastewater discharge according to any other method. This appears to prohibit the on-site use of GW.

However, officials verbally state that GW use is permitted where there is no wastewater network. The Ministry of Water and Irrigation has more than once looked at legislation to permit and regulate the use of GW, and in 2006, Jordan Standard JS1776 was published. Entitled *Greywater Reuse in Rural Areas*, this code does not fully clarify the position on GW use. The code contains a number of definitions and explains what GW use is. It lists some general requirements for the protection of health and safety, including specifying allowable water quality levels for GW. But the code does not provide information on how a household can apply and be permitted to use GW, what the application process is, whether there is a monitoring requirement, or what the relevant permitting authority is. It also does not define 'rural areas' or clarify whether GW use is permitted in non-rural areas or not. The language of the standard implies that each potential user has to demonstrate that his system will provide water that meets the quality standards, but does not specify how.

However, the publication of the code is a positive step, as it indicates that there is government interest in facilitating GW use. The code is an example of a statutory instrument being developed using the 1989 WHO guidelines, where control of water quality is seen as the prime means of mitigating risk. In countries with weak regulatory regimes and where local government agencies have capacity limitations, such a code is likely to hinder, rather than facilitate, the use of GW by placing permitting and monitoring burdens on the household.

Conclusion

Given the water supply restrictions and poverty in some areas of the MENA region, and the interest in GW use among communities and its promotion from many donor organizations, there is a lack of clear policies that would enable low-cost and straightforward GW use while providing the required risk mitigation. The following section looks at some elements such policies could address.

Framework for a policy

This section sets out some important issues specific to the MENA region, which should be addressed in policy.

Policy must balance the risks from controlled greywater use with the alternatives

Water policymakers in the MENA region have to address a number of competing issues. Priorities vary from country to country, but the goals of increasing economic growth, reducing poverty, protecting and improving health, protecting environmental resources, addressing food security, and maintaining internal and external security all have implications for water resource and supply management policy. While GW use carries risks, there are also risks to communities with inadequate water supplies. These include economic deprivation and malnutrition. The Stockholm Framework[2] allows the concept of relative risk, whereby the risks of both using and not using a particular intervention are considered together. The 2006 WHO guidelines allow that the tolerable burden of disease may vary from one country to another and suggests a flexible and contextually-derived approach to risk management. In other words, a practice which carries an unacceptable risk in one country, may actually reduce overall health risks in another country or at least carry a risk which is acceptable when balanced with the benefits that the practice brings. Each country must therefore address its own risk context. In some areas of MENA, this may mean that allowing GW use is the lesser evil, when compared to the results of water poverty particularly in low-income areas. The result may be that practices which are unacceptable in other countries are tolerated, or even promoted in some areas in the MENA region.

Policy must be integrated

A GW policy cannot stand alone, unrelated to other water usage and demand policies. Ideally, GW use should be set within an integrated part of a comprehensive water resources management framework. Policies on water supply, allocation, demand management, agricultural policy, and wastewater use should be linked and complementary. As an example, a country which has accepted the principle of wastewater use must consider where household GW use fits within this and decide how this particular wastewater resource can be used – at the household or under the control of the authorities. To prohibit use at the household, but then not to use it downstream, would go against a policy of recognizing its importance as a secondary water resource. Alternatively, a country with a highly-developed wastewater treatment-and-use policy and practice may want to restrict GW use in areas where total wastewater is captured and used centrally.

Policy should be simple and not disincentivize greywater use

The principle of simplicity and ease of implementation adopted by Arizona should be followed. If complex application requirements – such as form filling, presentation of drawings, system inspection, or water quality monitoring – are placed on households, there is unlikely to be significant uptake of regulated GW-use. Particularly in countries with weak regulatory regimes and where local authorities have limited capacity, a realistic and workable regime should be adopted, whereby the requirements placed on local authorities should be minimized as far as possible. Following Arizona's example, information and guidance on risk management by householders should be well publicized and the responsibility placed with the householders to manage the system. Perhaps some pre-approved treatment systems, relevant to the MENA countries could be pre-determined, removing the burden from householders from seeking out professional advice.

Risk management should be behaviour based, rather than technology or water-quality based

The new WHO guidelines move away from an exclusive focus on water quality. A realistic policy in a MENA country would allow means of risk mitigation such as drip irrigation, protective gloves for workers, and restrictions on GW usage and permitted crops, and may suggest requirements for food preparation and cooking of produce irrigated by GW. A policy which simply requires water quality to be of a particular standard will: 1) be too expensive to implement; 2) be too expensive to regulate; 3) not fully address all the important risks; 4) likely, paradoxically, be too conservative and restrictive. Each country should review the new WHO guidelines and seek to address these within the country context. Education of users should be an important target for policy makers.

Policy development should include stakeholders

Both Keough et al. and Laban (Chapters 8 and 7 respectively) in this volume argue strongly that insufficient involvement of the end users in the development of GW systems leads to non-optimal solutions. Policy developers should therefore take care to consult with and involve communities in developing policies which are appropriate, understandable, and workable at the community level. The context in low-income areas is likely to be different from that which the (generally more well-to-do) policy makers have experience in.

Policy must be clear regarding implementation

The new Jordanian Standard is an example of a GW regulatory tool developed without sufficient information as to how it should be implemented. Codes should set out clearly what potential users should do to satisfy the regulatory authorities. In the case of some (e.g. California), an application is to be made, with supporting information. In the case of Arizona, the user is automatically in compliance, provided certain basic conditions are met.

Policy should not place undue financial burdens on users

No one should be penalized for responsibly using GW. Expensive professional assistance should not be required, nor should the use of expensive materials be mandatory. Application fees (if any) should take into account that the purpose of GW policy is to provide additional water resource to water-stressed (and possibly low-income) populations, not a revenue raiser for local government. Some of the costs cited in earlier chapters suggest that the types of GW treatment units that are being proposed for the region are costly enough in themselves, without adding any extra expense.

Decentralized use should be considered for poor communities

Some countries in the MENA region have adopted a centralized approach to wastewater use, where wastewater is captured and treated centrally and is then distributed or sold for irrigation in large networks and schemes. This approach sometimes conflicts with the idea of decentralized use (of GW or blackwater) at household or even community level. Arguments against a decentralized approach include: 1) the need to control the treatment process to guarantee the treated effluent water quality and minimize health risks; 2) the need to control irrigation practices, also to minimize risk to both workers and end users of the irrigated product; 3) the need to maintain a certain flow in the wastewater network to transport the waste; 4) the need to maintain a particular concentration/dilution of effluent so as not to disrupt the wastewater treatment process, which was designed for a particular effluent concentration. However, centrally-treated wastewater is rarely returned and made available to the householders that produced it. In the context of alleviating community water scarcity, especially in low-income and rural areas, policy makers must recognise the importance of the locally managed GW resource, and not allow a centralizing tendency to over-rule.

Policy should differentiate with regard to scale

Many jurisdictions that have drawn up legislation for GW use have found it beneficial to differentiate between large and small users, since the implications of GW use in each case are different and the cost and complexity of solutions are also different. The 2007 Aqaba Meeting and the chapters in this book all address community use for agriculture. However, other applications of GW also may be addressed in a policy. Customers of a large hotel or high-rise building that uses the GW from residents and staff will expect a higher degree of protection than a single household reusing its own GW under its own control, where household pathogens are shared together anyway. One of the main purposes in large-usage legislation would be to provide for protection to health and environment and ensure the responsible design, installation, and operation of the GW system. Since large usage systems will combine GW from more than one household, additional treatment complexity, and therefore cost, will result.

By contrast, household systems, where GW is used solely within the property of the household, carry less risk and should be cheap and easy to install, maintain, and regulate. Policy should clearly address these contexts separately.

Conclusion

The conclusions to be drawn from the chapters in this book and this discussion on GW policy are often down-to-earth and derived from common sense. Donor-funded work in the region has demonstrated that GW is of interest as a means to supplement the amount of irrigation water available to communities, particularly in low-income areas. Regulatory agencies have been slow to address this. With workable treatment solutions available (although perhaps more work is needed to further reduce complexity and expense) and numerous demonstration schemes having been tried out, governments must address head-on the implications and risks. Within the context of their own water resources management policies and priorities, and taking into account the needs of (particularly) rural and low-come water-stressed users, authorities must examine the relative risks and benefits of allowing GW use and must take a view on the risk mitigation requirements that are necessary and workable in each context. On this basis, policies must be developed and communicated to the potential users, taking into account the cultural and religious values. The policies must then be implemented clearly and fairly. It is only after a number of years of consistent GW use on a larger scale that the success or otherwise of many of the treatment approaches discussed in this book, together with the environmental and health-related implications, can properly be evaluated against the benefits to the householders. Ultimately, the market will tease out the costs and benefits, and communities will take their own decisions on the effectiveness of GW use. But governments owe their citizens a clear policy framework, against which GW use can be implemented, examined, investigated, and discussed.

Notes

1. The Queensland Sewerage and Water Supply Act 1949–82.
2. An approach to risk assessment and risk management of water-related infectious diseases, developed following an expert meeting held in Stockholm by WHO in 2001.

References

Buildings Standards Commission (2007) *California Code of Regulations, Title 24, Part 5 – California Plumbing Code, Graywater Systems for Single Family Dwellings*. State of California, Sacremento.

Center for the Study of the Built Environment (CSBE) (2003) *Greywater Reuse in Other Countries and Its Applicability to Jordan* [online], available from: http://www.csbe.org/graywater/contents/htm [accessed 6 January 2009].

Jordanian Institute for Standards and Metrology (JSIM) (2008) *Jordan Standard, No 1776.2008, Water – Reclaimed grey water in rural areas*. Jordanian Institute for Standards and Metrology.

Lighthouse Sustainable Building Center (2007) *BC Green Building Code Background Research, Greywater Recycling* [online], available from: http://www.sustainablebuildingcentre.com [accessed 6 January 2009].

Mara, D. and Kramer, A. (2008) 'The 2006 WHO guidelines for wastewater and greywater use in agriculture: a practical interpretation', in I. Al Baz, R. Otterpohl and C. Wendland (eds), *Efficient Management of Wastewater: Its Treatment and Reuse in Water-Scarce Countries*, pp. 1–17, Springer, Berlin.

Ministry of Water and Irrigation, Jordan, (MWI) (1996) *Water Strategy for Jordan* [online], available from: http://www.mwi.gov.jo/mwi/WaterStrategy.aspx#WATER%20STRATEGY [accessed 6 January 2009].

Ministry of Public Works and Housing (1988) *Sanitary Wastewater System Code*, Ministry of Public Works and Housing, Amman, Jordan.

Oasis Design (2005) *Greywater Policy Packet* [online], available from: http://oasisdesign.net/downloads/GWPolicyPacket.pdf [accessed 6 January 2009].

Queensland's Department of Infrastructure and Planning, Plumbing and Building (2008) *Greywater* [online], available from: http://www.dip.qld.gov.au/sustainable-living/greywater.html [accessed 6 January 2009].

Redwood, M. (2008) 'The application of pilot research on greywater in the Middle East North Africa region (MENA)', *Journal of Environmental Studies* 65: 109–17.

World Health Organization (WHO) (1989) *Health Guidelines for the Use of Wastewater in Agriculture and Aquaculture* (Technical Report Series 778), WHO, Geneva.

WHO (2006) *Overview of Greywater Management Health Considerations* (Report WHO-EM/CEH/125/E).

About the author

Dr McIlwaine is a chartered engineer and the director of Centre for the Study of the Built Environment (CSBE). His experience and interests are primarily in the water and environment sectors, and he has carried out studies and projects in a number of countries in the Middle East, including environmental assessments, due diligence, policy and legal studies, strategic planning, and development consulting for the public and private sectors, as well as for donor clients. He carried out a study into greywater in Jordan in 2002–2003.

Email: mcilwaine@csbe.org

CHAPTER 12

Conclusion: Next steps for research, policy and implementation

Mark Redwood, Stephen McIlwaine and Marwan Owaygen

The issue of water scarcity will continue to dominate debates about the environment in the Middle East and North Africa (MENA). This is particularly so given the geopolitical context and the importance of water to national security. As supply options become more restricted, due to population growth, climate change, and the high cost of additional sources, the lack of available water will increasingly harm the real economy. It is also reasonable to assume that climate change will disproportionately impact those facing poverty and a lack of access to water. Despite this bleak scenario, there are potential ways to ease the burden of water scarcity in rural areas where existing supplies are insufficient. These include a shift towards demand management and the use of alternative sources of water such as greywater (GW).

We know that GW can provide a modest addition to national water budgets and should be counted as a part of an integrated water resource management (IWRM) strategy. The evidence presented in this book outlines the use of GW in low-income rural and urban areas as a method to mitigate some of the burden of poverty. Its value is particularly apparent in areas where there is little or no connection to the main sewerage or water provision networks. Also, and importantly in the MENA region, GW use need not contradict any fundamental tenets of environmental management suggested by Islam (see Al-Jayyousi in this volume, Chapter 10).

This book has discussed the details of three separate GW pilot schemes in Jordan and Palestine. Technical details of the treatment units have been provided, with an evaluation of each unit's performance in treating GW. In each case, with the assistance of donor support, GW systems have been installed and are providing additional water for use in irrigation of home gardens. The discussion in these chapters is technical with a focus on the quality of the water before and after treatment, although in each case, the importance of involving and training the local communities are discussed. Four other chapters discussed the importance and results of the beneficiaries' participation in the design and implementation of GW units and programmes. The purpose of this final section is to step back, make some observations and draw some conclusions from the analysis presented, and determine what remaining issues must be addressed by practitioners, development agencies, and policy makers in the region.

The dominance of the technological approach

The focus on the quality of the treated water as the main way to reduce health risks – as discussed by both Redwood (Introduction) and McIlwaine (Chapter 11) – has led to an engineering-dominated approach to GW treatment. The systems presented in this book are complicated and expensive, although they mostly produce good quality water. There are questions as to the appropriateness of such systems – which need user intervention in maintenance, require replacement of filter media, and incur ongoing energy costs for pumping – to treat water simply to irrigate plants in rural areas where untreated GW is often used anyway at very little cost.

There is also a misplaced optimism in the idea that technology can solve the environmental burdens that households and communities face, including water scarcity. There is no lack of technological options (for example, see EAWAG (2006)); but it is the adoption of these technologies which continues to face huge social and economic obstacles. Some of the difficulties were outlined in Laban's chapter in this volume (Chapter 7). Our understanding of the social and economic issues associated with GW use is limited, despite the considerable case examples that have been gathered. The promise of technology in the field of wastewater treatment and management has frequently failed to live up to expectations.

The imposition of solutions from outside

Researchers frequently make the erroneous assumption that a good idea from, say, an environmental standpoint will be adopted simply because it is a 'good' idea. In fact simple ways to improve their economic and social standing are far more important to people. This explains why many ideas that may be detrimental to a society, village, or collective end up being adopted regardless, particularly in the absence of strong governance. Put simply, individuals and households seek increased opportunities and this motivation competes with, and often wins over, social and community obligations when it comes to environmental resources. What this suggests is the paramount importance of governments coming to terms with wastewater use, and GW use in particular, by developing a policy that balances the benefits of its use with a management of its risks.

The notion that social and economic standing trump environmental goodwill in some cases strengthens the argument for abandoning large investments in socially unproven technology until there is a clear marketable incentive. The fact is that many income-generating ideas that are environmentally detrimental will be adopted just as readily as ideas that benefit a community at some economic sacrifice. Several chapters explore these triggers, but we are in agreement that more work is required. Until there is more clarity on the economic benefit of GW use, we would caution against widespread investment in household-level treatment where dependence on outside funding is a core component of the business model. In this regard, many of the chapters in this book are perhaps overly optimistic with respect to the treatment and use of GW. This optimism is not yet anchored in strong evidence that there are economic incentives for households to adopt GW use.

Conflicts with national policy

Given the importance of wastewater recovery as a component of water management in the region, it is important to differentiate between the perspectives of governments and the perspectives of households with respect to the treatment and use of GW. At the national level, and particularly in water-scarce countries, the value of GW is expected to reduce the deficit of water and to contribute positively to the enhancement of national security with respect to water reserves. Given this intrinsic value of water, governments might decide to invest in wastewater even if it is not financially justifiable. Such a subsidy reflects the belief that other non-financial dimensions of wastewater management are important (e.g. sustainable use of underground water or preservation of precious underground freshwater). In other words, governments might see wider reasons to invest in GW than the strictly financial ones.

Training and awareness

The viability of using treated GW at the household level depends on the classic sustainable development balance between four concepts: economic, social, environmental/health and to some extent institutional. Some chapters in this volume focus on the importance of training and awareness. While training and awareness are critical, a problem exists when economic incentives are lacking. Investing heavily in training and awareness is unlikely to lead to a greater acceptance of GW if the economic rewards are uncertain at best. It is thus our view that GW use – and the training and awareness associated with it – should become a part of a larger approach to water conservation in general. Instead of donor-supported initiatives at the household level (which, in our view, are not proving to be financially sustainable despite a high level of interest), we are more inclined to suggest that awareness-raising be concentrated in the traditional places of learning – schools and mosques – and through agricultural extension. The religious and cultural emphasis on environmental protection in the region is a perspective that will encourage more acceptance of the practice.

Financial and economic feasibility

Most of the chapters included in this volume illustrate a keen interest in options to use wastewater at the household level. However, there is a strong need to further investigate the economic feasibility of this reuse. Further analysis would require detail on all types of associated costs and benefits. Some of these costs would include the costs of separation of grey- and black-wastewater, construction costs of treatment units, operational and maintenance costs of these units, and the costs of agricultural inputs and infrastructure – drip irrigation systems, greenhouses, etc. The benefits would include the value of crops produced and any savings made from emptying cesspits and septic tanks. The costs and benefits should then be compared with the realistic alternatives to this type of GW use.

The use of treated GW in home gardens would be economically viable under three conditions: 1) benefits exceed costs where 'time' is taken into consideration as a key variable; 2) the positive difference between benefits and costs is significant as a percentage of household income; 3) this difference is significantly higher compared with the difference between benefits and costs associated with the use of other water sources (e.g. water purchased from tankers). It would also be important in future research to investigate the economic viability of restricted irrigation (and corresponding treatment systems) versus unrestricted irrigation (and corresponding treatment systems). Two further questions are pertinent in any new research on this topic. First, is it worth investing in a treatment system that would allow unrestricted irrigation compared with a system that would allow only for restricted food crops? Second, what is the minimum land size needed at the household level to make the use of treated GW in agriculture economically viable?

Greywater use as an interim option for particularly marginalized households

Marginalized households who are deprived of other sources of water, who cannot afford to buy freshwater, who are currently using untreated GW in irrigation and incurring health costs, and who are also facing serious food security problems are most likely to benefit from treated GW. In this context, the use of treated GW at household level for home consumption may be a promising strategy for the much-marginalized communities to enhance their food security, especially in the presence of high food prices. In this case, training and awareness would be central to reducing the health risks that would result from a low-performing treatment system or from an inappropriate use of the treated water. Whatever the case, there is a strong argument to limit support for GW to its use as an interim measure before alternate water sources can be found or until treatment is manageable. The promotion of the use of treated GW in home gardens as a pro-poor strategy might become less realistic and more complicated as we move from home-consumed crops to commercialized crops and from informal/unregulated practice to a formal/controlled practice where public health and regulatory mechanisms become critical issues. Also, none of these arguments would arise if the authorities would provide an adequate supply of water to each household.

The institutional setting

Institutional aspects are also critical. The challenge facing policy makers is whether or not to legalize GW use when it is difficult to employ monitoring mechanisms that can verify compliance with legislation. This is particularly the case when GW is managed at the household level. Public health is naturally the central issue for most governments, and crops for market use are usually scrutinized more closely than crops destined for household consumption. Further thinking is required on the importance of centralized public large-scale GW treatment plants (GWTP) versus small-scale decentralized and privately owned greywater treatment units at household level. Large-scale collective GWTP would ensure higher and more standardized GW quality, be easier to monitor, and provide flexibility in pricing the water in such a way to ensure some cost recovery of the treatment plants (construction and operational costs). Nor would a semi-collective treatment and use scheme deprive users from the needed economic incentives.

Don't over-regulate

This volume offers up a series of chapters that are very optimistic on the possibility that GW can offer substantial economic and social rewards if it is used as a supplement to freshwater. As often noted in the literature, GW use is safe under controlled conditions (WHO, 2006; EAWAG, 2006) and the key to these controlled conditions is to manage the influent. To achieve these controlled conditions, very little investment or effort is required. Policy on this point, as noted by McIlwaine in this volume (Chapter 11), must be pragmatic and well integrated into national IWRM policies. So while the potential for GW to make a contribution to freshwater conservation exists, we also would issue a plea for pragmatism. It is clear, and there are ample examples included in the chapters in this volume, that unsanctioned GW use does happen and is a fact of water use in the MENA region. Moreover, government intervention is minimal or non-existent in some of these projects. To increase engagement, we are clearly in need of more economic data to understand the financial dimensions of household GW use.

Are governments willing to invest? The decentralization versus centralization debate

Widespread government investment schemes in GW treatment and use have been almost nonexistent. In fact, most GW use takes place with regulators either turning a blind eye or simply not knowing that the practice is taking place. The preference for governments has been to expand conventional collection and treatment throughout all populated areas, both urban and rural. A key question arises from this: would governments be willing to invest significant resources in infrastructure to collect raw GW and treat and distribute treated GW to users for agricultural purposes? If so, the opportunities of scale would significantly alter the cost–benefit balance.

Conclusions from the work

Taking the above into account, we come to several conclusions with regard to how to proceed in managing household GW:

- Where conventional collection and treatment systems exist, widespread GW use should *not* be promoted, partly due to the network system designs that rely on a certain amount of water flow to transport the waste solids, and because of the impact of more concentrated influent on the process at the treatment works.
- The market for GW irrigated foods needs to be managed carefully. This requires: 1) information and knowledge on the products; 2) training for farmers on how to minimize risks associated with GW use (premised on the WHO guidelines); 3) controls and monitoring.
- For future wastewater management systems, GW use at the local level should be incorporated into the overall management concept. This means firstly, evaluating how the GW will be used, secondly, what the potential economic benefits are for its use, and thirdly, the implication of the existing systems for uses of wastewater. This demand-centric approach should govern all investments in wastewater management.
- A decentralized approach is important, but household treatment approaches are not proving to be feasible from the standpoint of monitoring despite some promising case examples.
- If GW use is only financially feasible following external support for the capital expenditure, then other solutions should be considered.
- The WHO guidelines on wastewater use should be the benchmark for any new policy development on GW use. Policy should be pragmatic, simple and reflect a reasonable effort to minimize direct contact with GW.

What happens next?

If GW use is to be adopted widely, it cannot be done so through case-by-case donor-funded projects. The sustainability of these projects is not proven despite the promising research results in some cases. It is essential that any further investments in this sector address a fundamental tenet of design: close collaboration with users in the design and development process.

A second fundamental requirement is to better compile and assess the economic data required for increased adoption of GW at the household and community levels. Public investment in the development of a better understanding of the economic costs and benefits of GW – specifically in the quantitative assessment of externalities – would likely help shift interest towards more action in support of the idea. Unfortunately, aside from case examples, to date there appears to be no significant research that we could find in the MENA region where a strong economic analysis had been carried out, taking into account externalities and a rigorous assessment of the social benefits. If household uptake of treatment is not self-financing, then a targeted subsidy is an alternate possibility. However, we would argue for a targeted subsidy only in the case where there is a clear societal benefit, something that has yet to be proven.

Third, renewed research is required, but we would argue not on technological options – there are many proven techniques – but rather on markets, attitudes, and household requirements. What is then required is a revolutionary approach among entrepreneurs who will take the cause of household GW management and offer associated services for profit, enabled to do so by policy. Technologists could then help promote this uptake in a feasible manner. It is far from certain, however, that this decentralized approach to operation and implementation of GW would be welcome in the highly centralized political economy of the MENA region.

References

Swiss Federal Institute of Aquatic Science and Technology (EAWAG) (2006) *Greywater Management in Low and Middle-Income Countries*, EAWAG, Dubendorf.

World Health Organisation (WHO) (2006) *Guidelines for the Safe Use of Wastewater, Excreta and Greywater* (vols 1–4), WHO, Geneva.

About the authors

Mark Redwood is a programme leader for the Urban Poverty and Environment (UPE) initiative at IDRC. He is a specialist on environmental issues with a specific focus on urban water management and urban agriculture. Since 2002, he has developed and managed most of IDRC's projects related to urban agriculture and wastewater recycling. His regions of work included Sub-Saharan Africa, the Middle East, and North Africa. He holds a Master's in Urban Planning from McGill University and has contributed to numerous publications, conferences, and peer-review journals on the topic of urban agriculture.
Email; mredwood@idrc.ca

Dr Stephen McIlwaine is the director of CSBE, with interest and experience in a variety of water and environment issues in the Middle East.

Dr Marwan Owaygen is an economist who specialized in environmental economics. He works as a Senior Program Officer with Canada's International Development Research Centre in the Cairo regional office.

Index

ablution 63–6, 78, 142
acceptability 101–10
acceptance 53, 83–4, 102–4, 119, 133, 167
   see also community; public
aerobic filter 7, 19, 24–5
agriculture 19, 24, 26, 37, 55, 102
   see also garden; greywater, in; irrigation; PARC; urban; wastewater, in
algae 4, 22
Amman 2, 30, 38–40, 57, 113–5
analysis, cost-benefit *see* cost
Aqaba declaration 10, 57, 101, 152, 157, 161
aquaculture 4, 153
aquifer/s 89, 114
Arizona 1, 8–9, 153, 155–6, 159–60
Australia 1, 7–9, 79, 151, 156

bacteria 3, 24, 132
barrel *see* four-barrel
bathroom 2, 32, 62, 154, 156
Bedouins 60, 77
beneficiary/ies 37–41, 47–54, 104–6, 122–4, 144, 165
   female 129–34
   see also household
bidet *see* toilet/s
bills *see* water
blackwater 25, 30, 52, 78, 110, 155
   separation of 9, 36–7, 59, 64, 83, 89–97
   use of 103–4, 160
blockage 48, 121, 155–6

California 1, 153–4, 160
capacity-building 53, 55, 77–9, 82, 119
CBOs (community based organizations) 53, 60–3, 77–82

cesspit
   emptying 22–3, 29–30, 38, 102, 133–5, 168
   management 17, 25
   systems 89–97
   see cesspools; septic tank
cesspools 52, 59, 64, 78, 83
chemical/s 6, 155
   see also COD
chromium 41–3
climate 3, 7, 141, 165
clogging 22, 24, 35, 48–9
coal 19–20
COD (chemical oxygen demand) 6, 21–3, 40–3, 66–71, 84, 102
committee 37, 53, 61, 73, 80–5, 130–6
   see also LSC; PARC
community
   acceptance 125
   development 10, 37, 117, 119
   engagement 113, 119, 122, 125
   involvement 18, 78, 82, 107, 114, 119–22
   knowledge 82, 85
   participation 53–4, 60–1, 114, 117, 119, 125
   see also CBOs; peri-urban; rural communities
compost 39, 43, 109
conservation 1, 115, 120, 139, 142, 145–6
   see also water
constraints 48, 56, 61, 82, 107, 117
construction 34–6, 46–9, 68–71, 77, 80–5, 118
   cost 19, 92–6, 104, 168–9
consultation 10, 23, 60, 85, 107, 116
consumption 19, 24–5, 45, 105, 130, 168–9
   see also water

contamination 2, 4–5, 24, 29, 45, 132
cost 49–51, 92, 115
    -benefit analysis/ratio 9–10, 72, 91, 152
    recovery 90–1, 115, 123, 126, 169
    see also construction; low-cost; maintenance; O&M; operational costs
crops 6, 9, 109, 134–6, 159, 168–9
    see also garden; industrial crops; irrigation, of; vegetable/s
culture 103, 132, 139–40

decomposition 44–6
demand management *see* WDM
desalination 1, 3, 114
disease 4, 39, 158
disposal 17, 41, 68, 83, 108, 132–3
    see also greywater; wastewater
drinking water 62, 102, 132
drippers 24, 44, 47
drip irrigation 24, 47–50, 102, 133, 154–5, 168
Dublin Principles 3, 116, 139

economic
    benefit 9–10, 52, 123–7, 151, 167, 170
    feasibility 35, 56, 89, 113, 122, 168
effluent 23–5, 38, 67, 70–1, 104–5, 157
    quality 8, 47, 84, 90–2, 102, 160–1
    see also greywater; wastewater
electric pump 35, 47, 133
energy 9, 19, 24–5, 105, 123, 144, 166
empowerment *see* women's
environmental impact 6, 19, 24, 36, 47, 53
excreta 4, 89–90, 154–8
exposure 4–5, 153

faecal coliform 4, 23, 45
faeces 78, 103
farmers 2, 56, 104–9, 118, 170

feasibility 38, 51, 59–60, 104–5, 118, 152
    see also economic
fertilizer 2, 46
filtration 20, 34, 155
flies 22, 121–3
food
    production 1, 21, 25–6
    security 18, 73, 118, 129, 158, 168
    see also training
four-barrel 29, 31–42, 47–50, 118–9
framework 4–5, 60, 119–20, 139–41, 158–9, 162
freshwater 6, 18, 106, 118, 142, 167–9
    conservation *or* saving 31, 52, 57, 133
fruit trees 18–24, 39, 103, 121, 130, 155
funding 18, 89–91, 95–7, 104, 120, 167

garden 121, 124, 152
    agriculture 21–2, 35, 38–43, 48, 106
    crops 29–30, 38–9, 41, 45, 55
    irrigation 52, 89–96, 104–6, 156
    see also home garden
gender 108, 116, 119, 123–4, 129–137
gravel media 35, 48–50
grease 19–20, 34, 48–9, 65–7
greywater (GW)
    disposal 9, 31, 154
    effluent 6, 23, 36, 41, 43, 47
    in agriculture 6, 18–9, 22, 25–6, 91, 139–44
    management policies 59–60
    plumbing 155–7
    quality 39–43, 59–66
    separation 9, 30, 50, 57, 63, 78, 168
    technology 101–10, 113, 133
    see also greywater treatment; household
greywater treatment 6, 129, 156, 168–9
    in Palestine 17–26, 91
    in Jordan 30–4, 50, 56, 68, 73

groundwater 1, 3, 89–90, 142, 155
   pollution 17, 30, 62, 95
   resources 23, 52
guidelines *see* principles; WHO

harvesting 5, 45, 68, 144
   see also water
health
   and environment 110, 125, 161
   -based targets 4, 7
   problems 22–3, 151
   risk 2, 4–5, 154, 156
   see also public; WHO
home garden 22, 35, 38–43, 48, 106
household
   beneficiaries 17, 29, 55, 119–1
   greywater 43, 113–27
   income 3, 17–8, 36, 73, 168
   waste 108–10
   see also low-income
housewives 47, 78–9, 82, 110

IDRC (International Development
   Research Centre) 30–6, 61, 91,
   113–6, 129, 151
impact 53, 82, 101–2, 120, 165, 170
   of GW systems 17–8, 25, 37–9,
      45, 94, 105
   on soil 6, 22, 41
   on women 129–31
   see also environmental impact
impurities 30, 142–3
incentives 7, 167–9
income 54, 83, 94, 108, 115–8,
   129–36
   rate 62–4
   see also household; low-income
indicators 3, 50, 79, 118, 130
industrial crops 65, 71
infection 4, 39
influent 6, 23, 52, 169–70
insects 22, 48, 83
inspection 35, 49, 159
installation 25, 35, 104–5, 116, 133,
   136
   and operation 114, 161
   of GWT units 19, 23, 37–8, 52,
      118–9, 156–7
   systems 50, 119, 121–3

intervention 5, 106, 123–5, 144,
   158, 166–9
   see also technology
interviews 80, 82, 116, 131–3, 136
INWRDAM (Inter-Islamic Network
   on Water Resources Development
   and Management) 30–8, 47, 53–7,
   81, 114–6, 120
irrigation
   agricultural 90, 95, 103
   of crops 25, 31, 47, 153–4
   networks 20, 24, 47–9
   supplementary 29, 40
   systems 25–6, 154, 156
   see also drip irrigation; gar-
      den; greywater; restricted
      irrigation
Islam 10, 78, 103, 116, 139–45, 165
Islamic law *or* principles 8, 139–45
Israel 1–3, 114
IWRM (Integrated Water Resource
   Management) 9–10, 55, 139, 165,
   169

Karak, Jordan 29–57, 61, 113–8,
   124–6
kitchen/s 2, 6, 64–5, 83, 133, 154

laundry 2–6, 30, 142, 154–6
law *see* Islamic law
Lebanon 30, 114, 129–37
low-cost 2, 25, 41, 56, 101, 104
low-income 37, 43, 109, 120, 151,
   158–61
   households 6, 29–31, 36, 126
LSC (local stakeholder committee)
   37, 59–62, 79, 81, 86, 119

maintenance 35, 47, 68, 78, 84–5,
   90, 103, 144
   cost/s 18, 25, 93–6, 105–6, 115,
      168
   see also O&M
management strategy 3, 30, 61, 73
manure 39, 43, 108–9
medical 23, 39
MENA (Middle East and North
   Africa region) 1–10, 29–30, 56,
   110–7, 151–71

mitigation 2, 5, 130
    see also risk mitigation
monitoring 18, 29, 38, 42–4, 107,
    169–70
    and evaluation 18, 119–20
    requirement 153–9
    survey 53–5, 120–4
    systems 26, 125
mosquitoes 22, 26, 121–3, 155
mulching 39, 43–7
Muslim 78, 116, 141–3

networks 62–4, 82–3, 108, 118, 132,
    153
    see also INWRDAM; irrigation;
        sewerage; wastewater
NGOs (non governmental organi-
    zations) 25, 60–3, 77–82, 89–91,
    108, 131
    local 53, 119
nickel 41–3
nitrogen 4, 21, 45–7, 65–9, 108, 142
NPV (net present value) 50–1, 94–5
nutrient/s 2–4, 45–6, 57, 65, 95

O&M (operation and maintenance)
    18–9, 36–7, 54–5, 93–5, 122–4
    costs 49–50
odour 22–4, 35–6, 68, 83–4, 119,
    121
    control *or* reduction 10, 23, 41,
        47
olive 29, 36–46, 50, 56, 72–3, 87
OMAN 90–1, 96, 103
operation *see* O&M
operational costs 51, 92–3, 104, 169
    see also O&M
organic
    load 2, 20
    matter 6, 26, 30, 39, 41–6, 67
organizations *see* CBOs; NGOs;
    WHO

Palestine 17–26, 30, 89–97, 101–5,
    165
    see also greywater treatment;
        PARC; Qebia Village; rural
        communities

PARC (Palestinian Agricultural Relief
    Committees) 30, 91, 102
participation 37, 60–1, 73, 78, 107,
    114
    see also community; public;
        stakeholders
participatory
    approach 72, 85, 110, 113–27
    development communication
        (PDC) 61, 79
    rapid (*or* rural) appraisal (PRA)
        59, 61, 77–8, 107
    see also PTD
pathogens 2–4, 26, 68, 102, 153, 161
    removal 67, 73, 84, 102
performance 18–9, 25, 47, 91, 123,
    156, 165
    of septic tank *or* UASB 67, 71–3,
        102
peri-urban
    communities 36, 53, 89–91,
        113, 118
    poor 1, 29 , 90, 118
    wastewater 115–6
permaculture 38–9, 46, 56
phosphorous 4, 45, 65, 142
piping systems 92, 96, 104
PLAN:NET Ltd 31, 35, 79, 86, 113
plant growth 4, 43–5, 142
plants 6, 22–3, 29, 142, 155, 166
    and soils 38–9, 41–6, 54
    see also wastewater treatment
plumbing 19, 155–7
    see also greywater
policy makers 3–4, 18, 143–5, 151–2,
    160–1, 166
pollutants 6, 24, 40
    see also groundwater; soil
poor *see* peri-urban
population growth 1, 29, 89, 165
potable water 2, 29, 50, 93, 156
poverty
    alleviation 57, 115, 144, 158
    reduction 30, 57, 113
pre-treatment 7, 34–5, 48
price/s 3, 35–6, 49–51, 115, 118, 168
principles 55, 116–7
    see also Dublin Principles;
        Islamic law *or* principles

privatization 113–5, 123, 126
productivity 31, 38–9, 43, 72
public
 acceptance 7–10
 health 26–9, 37, 59–62, 79, 113, 122
 participation 36, 59–60, 116
 perception 8, 25, 89, 91, 95–6, 104
pump 19, 24–5, 34, 48–50, 70, 121–2
 trucks 25, 136
 see also electric pump
PTD (Participatory Technology Development) 101–9

Qebia Village, Palestine 17–26, 105
Queensland 156–7
questionnaire 17, 19–21, 38, 78, 91–2, 131
Quran 140–2

rain 18, 36, 39–40, 49, 118, 155
regulations 64, 67–9, 80–1, 84, 90, 152–6
regulatory approach 151–62
restricted irrigation 31, 41, 47–8, 65–7, 73, 84, 168
risk mitigation *or* management 5, 151, 153, 158–61
rural communities 10, 56, 102, 110, 131, 151
 in Jordan 59–60, 73, 78, 81–3
 in Palestine 89, 91

salinity *see* soil
sand filters 6–7, 19–20, 59, 67–73, 80–5, 102
 see also septic tank
sanitation 1–2, 4, 8, 60, 114
 decentralized 95–6
 expenditure 92, 94
 facilities 78, 89–90
savings 2–3, 38, 50, 108, 121, 168
scarcity *see* water scarcity
septic tank 24, 97, 118, 157, 168
 pumping out 30, 50, 121
 sand filter *or* intermittent sand filter 59, 67–73, 80, 84–5

up-flow gravel system 19–21, 73, 90–1, 102
sewage 4, 30, 40, 129, 132, 155
sewerage 1, 89, 114–5, 156, 165
 networks 29–30, 36, 59
showers 64–5, 78, 83, 103, 154–5
sinks 19, 24, 78, 89, 103, 154–7
sodium 41, 45
soil
 pollution 19, 24, 26
 properties 6, 41
 salinity 44–6, 119
 sampling 17, 38, 41, 45
 see also plants, and; impact on
stakeholders 7, 53–5, 116, 130, 134, 160
 participation 77–86
 see also LSC
strategy 8–9, 57, 108, 119, 125, 165–8
 see also management strategy
sustainability 9, 85, 91, 107, 137–9, 143
 of projects 53, 77, 122–4, 129, 132, 170
 long-term 54, 113

Tafila, Jordan 30–6, 48, 61, 118
tankers 17, 23, 36, 90, 118, 168
 see also water
Tannoura, Lebanon 129–36
technologies 7–10, 78–80, 101–10, 114, 126–7, 166
technology 84, 118, 140, 143, 159, 166
 interventions 57
 transfer 81, 122–5
 see also greywater; PTD
toilet/s 2, 30, 62–5, 83, 89, 103
 flushing 10, 133, 154–7
 wastewater 4, 19–21, 78, 90, 154
training 25, 53–5, 103, 109, 117, 119–25
 and awareness 77, 167–70
 and education 10, 18
 courses 77–85, 165
 on food processing 134–6
 workshop 59–61, 70, 73
trees *see* fruit trees; olive

UASB (up-flow anaerobic sludge
  blanket) 59, 67–70, 73, 80, 84, 102
  see also performance
up-flow anaerobic gravel filter 24–5
  see also septic tank
urban
  agriculture 30, 115, 137
  areas 30, 152, 165
  see peri-urban
urine 78, 103, 108–9, 156

valuation 92, 126
value *see* NPV
vegetable/s 18, 21, 23–4, 71, 103,
  134–5
  crops 104, 123

washing 34, 49, 63–8, 78, 142, 153–5
  machine 19, 40, 78, 154, 156
waste 9, 39, 46, 126, 139, 145, 170
  see also household; toilet/s
wastewater 1–2, 4, 8, 89–91, 139
  collection 59, 64, 83, 90, 96,
    153
  disposal 23, 59, 62, 90, 136
  effluent 30–1, 78
  in agriculture 153–4
  management 18, 25, 60–3, 73,
    82, 167, 170
  network 157, 161
  use 41, 81, 103–4, 151–2,
    157–60, 166
  see also peri-urban; toilet/s
wastewater treatment 40, 57, 115,
  159, 161, 166
  and use 18, 61, 64, 72, 85, 104
  plants 52, 90, 97, 157
  system 101, 155
water
  availability 1, 29, 115, 121, 133
  bills 25, 50, 72, 104, 121

budgets 1, 3, 165
conservation 2–3, 8, 82, 102,
  119, 167
consumption 21, 31, 37, 50, 72,
  93, 104
harvesting 18, 46
management 18, 21–5, 107,
  113–6, 123–33, 139–41
quality 4–8, 23–5, 38, 123, 144,
  153–7
resource 30, 72–3, 111, 158–60,
  165
shortages 26, 43, 54–5
sources 26, 36, 62, 151, 168
stress 1, 132
tankers 72, 83
see also blackwater; drinking
  water; freshwater; greywater; groundwater;
  INWRDAM; IWRM; potable
  water; wastewater; water scarcity; WDM
water scarcity 17, 55–7, 61–4, 101,
  129, 161, 165
WDM (water-demand management)
  3, 30, 55, 73, 136, 151
wetlands 1, 5–7, 9, 80, 84
WHO (World Health Organization)
  guidelines 2–8, 23–4, 29–31, 40–1,
  65–7, 153–60
women's
  cooperatives 18, 25, 55, 134
  empowerment 113, 124, 129–37
  roles 10, 21, 54–5, 107–9, 116,
    121–4
World Bank 115, 118, 129

yield 38, 43–5, 109

zeolite 67–8, 70–3, 102